CAREER EXAMINATION SERIES

MW00803789

THIS IS YOUR **PASSBOOK**® FOR ...

ASSOCIATE INVESTIGATOR

NATIONAL LEARNING CORPORATION®
passbooks.com

PASSBOOK® SERIES

THE *PASSBOOK® SERIES* has been created to prepare applicants and candidates for the ultimate academic battlefield – the examination room.

At some time in our lives, each and every one of us may be required to take an examination – for validation, matriculation, admission, qualification, registration, certification, or licensure.

Based on the assumption that every applicant or candidate has met the basic formal educational standards, has taken the required number of courses, and read the necessary texts, the *PASSBOOK® SERIES* furnishes the one special preparation which may assure passing with confidence, instead of failing with insecurity. Examination questions – together with answers – are furnished as the basic vehicle for study so that the mysteries of the examination and its compounding difficulties may be eliminated or diminished by a sure method.

This book is meant to help you pass your examination provided that you qualify and are serious in your objective.

The entire field is reviewed through the huge store of content information which is succinctly presented through a provocative and challenging approach – the question-and-answer method.

A climate of success is established by furnishing the correct answers at the end of each test.

You soon learn to recognize types of questions, forms of questions, and patterns of questioning. You may even begin to anticipate expected outcomes.

You perceive that many questions are repeated or adapted so that you can gain acute insights, which may enable you to score many sure points.

You learn how to confront new questions, or types of questions, and to attack them confidently and work out the correct answers.

You note objectives and emphases, and recognize pitfalls and dangers, so that you may make positive educational adjustments.

Moreover, you are kept fully informed in relation to new concepts, methods, practices, and directions in the field.

You discover that you arre actually taking the examination all the time: you are preparing for the examination by "taking" an examination, not by reading extraneous and/or supererogatory textbooks.

In short, this PASSBOOK®, used directedly, should be an important factor in helping you to pass your test.

ASSOCIATE INVESTIGATOR

JOB DESCRIPTION

This class of positions encompasses the conduct and supervision of investigations of varying degrees of difficulty. There are two assignment levels within this class of positions. All personnel perform related work. The following are typical assignments within this class of positions.

EXAMPLES OF TYPICAL TASKS

ASSIGNMENT LEVEL I

Under general supervision, with latitude for independent initiative and judgment, performs professional work of more than ordinary difficulty in the field of investigation. Assists in the supervision of subordinate staff. Reviews case records and reports and based thereon, makes recommendations as to action to be taken. May be regularly assigned to investigations which are of more than ordinary difficulty by reason of greater complexity or hazard. May make emergency and special investigations. Advises subordinates on difficult matters and interprets rules, regulations and codes for them. In the absence of supervisor, may assume the duties of that positions for a temporary period of time.

ASSTGNMENTLEVEL II

Under directions, with wide latitude for independent initiative and judgment in charge of a unit performing professional work in the field of investigation. Supervises subordinate personnel engaged in the conduct of routine and complex investigations. Interprets policy for the guidance of subordinate investigating staff. Issues orders and instructions to implement departmental directives. Serves as case consultant in the investigation of difficult cases. Conducts special investigations. Prepares reports and recommendations for administrative action. Plans and coordinates investigation schedules and assignments. Supervises training programs and conducts staff meetings. Prepares written reports. Testifies at hearings and in court. Serves as principal assistant to the head of a large or highly specialized unit performing routine, complex and very complex investigations. In the absence of supervisor, may assume the duties of that position for a temporary period of time.

SCOPE OF THE WRITTEN TEST

The written test will be of the multiple-choice type and may include questions on principles and techniques of investigations; criminal procedures; analytical skills to identify and evaluate problems; organizational skills to plan and schedule activities; comprehension and preparation of written materials; interpersonal relations; staff supervision and training; standards of employe conduct and other related areas including written communication; planning and organizing; sensitivity; analysis; judgment; decisiveness; work standards; behavioral flexibility; and technical translation.

HOW TO TAKE A TEST

I. YOU MUST PASS AN EXAMINATION

A. *WHAT EVERY CANDIDATE SHOULD KNOW*

Examination applicants often ask us for help in preparing for the written test. What can I study in advance? What kinds of questions will be asked? How will the test be given? How will the papers be graded?

As an applicant for a civil service examination, you may be wondering about some of these things. Our purpose here is to suggest effective methods of advance study and to describe civil service examinations.

Your chances for success on this examination can be increased if you know how to prepare. Those "pre-examination jitters" can be reduced if you know what to expect. You can even experience an adventure in good citizenship if you know why civil service exams are given.

B. *WHY ARE CIVIL SERVICE EXAMINATIONS GIVEN?*

Civil service examinations are important to you in two ways. As a citizen, you want public jobs filled by employees who know how to do their work. As a job seeker, you want a fair chance to compete for that job on an equal footing with other candidates. The best-known means of accomplishing this two-fold goal is the competitive examination.

Exams are widely publicized throughout the nation. They may be administered for jobs in federal, state, city, municipal, town or village governments or agencies.

Any citizen may apply, with some limitations, such as the age or residence of applicants. Your experience and education may be reviewed to see whether you meet the requirements for the particular examination. When these requirements exist, they are reasonable and applied consistently to all applicants. Thus, a competitive examination may cause you some uneasiness now, but it is your privilege and safeguard.

C. *HOW ARE CIVIL SERVICE EXAMS DEVELOPED?*

Examinations are carefully written by trained technicians who are specialists in the field known as "psychological measurement," in consultation with recognized authorities in the field of work that the test will cover. These experts recommend the subject matter areas or skills to be tested; only those knowledges or skills important to your success on the job are included. The most reliable books and source materials available are used as references. Together, the experts and technicians judge the difficulty level of the questions.

Test technicians know how to phrase questions so that the problem is clearly stated. Their ethics do not permit "trick" or "catch" questions. Questions may have been tried out on sample groups, or subjected to statistical analysis, to determine their usefulness.

Written tests are often used in combination with performance tests, ratings of training and experience, and oral interviews. All of these measures combine to form the best-known means of finding the right person for the right job.

II. HOW TO PASS THE WRITTEN TEST

A. NATURE OF THE EXAMINATION

To prepare intelligently for civil service examinations, you should know how they differ from school examinations you have taken. In school you were assigned certain definite pages to read or subjects to cover. The examination questions were quite detailed and usually emphasized memory. Civil service exams, on the other hand, try to discover your present ability to perform the duties of a position, plus your potentiality to learn these duties. In other words, a civil service exam attempts to predict how successful you will be. Questions cover such a broad area that they cannot be as minute and detailed as school exam questions.

In the public service similar kinds of work, or positions, are grouped together in one "class." This process is known as *position-classification*. All the positions in a class are paid according to the salary range for that class. One class title covers all of these positions, and they are all tested by the same examination.

B. FOUR BASIC STEPS

1) Study the announcement

How, then, can you know what subjects to study? Our best answer is: "Learn as much as possible about the class of positions for which you've applied." The exam will test the knowledge, skills and abilities needed to do the work.

Your most valuable source of information about the position you want is the official exam announcement. This announcement lists the training and experience qualifications. Check these standards and apply only if you come reasonably close to meeting them.

The brief description of the position in the examination announcement offers some clues to the subjects which will be tested. Think about the job itself. Review the duties in your mind. Can you perform them, or are there some in which you are rusty? Fill in the blank spots in your preparation.

Many jurisdictions preview the written test in the exam announcement by including a section called "Knowledge and Abilities Required," "Scope of the Examination," or some similar heading. Here you will find out specifically what fields will be tested.

2) Review your own background

Once you learn in general what the position is all about, and what you need to know to do the work, ask yourself which subjects you already know fairly well and which need improvement. You may wonder whether to concentrate on improving your strong areas or on building some background in your fields of weakness. When the announcement has specified "some knowledge" or "considerable knowledge," or has used adjectives like "beginning principles of..." or "advanced ... methods," you can get a clue as to the number and difficulty of questions to be asked in any given field. More questions, and hence broader coverage, would be included for those subjects which are more important in the work. Now weigh your strengths and weaknesses against the job requirements and prepare accordingly.

3) Determine the level of the position

Another way to tell how intensively you should prepare is to understand the level of the job for which you are applying. Is it the entering level? In other words, is this the position in which beginners in a field of work are hired? Or is it an intermediate or advanced level? Sometimes this is indicated by such words as "Junior" or "Senior" in the class title. Other jurisdictions use Roman numerals to designate the level – Clerk I, Clerk II, for example. The word "Supervisor" sometimes appears in the title. If the level is not indicated by the title, check the description of duties. Will you be working under very close supervision, or will you have responsibility for independent decisions in this work?

4) Choose appropriate study materials

Now that you know the subjects to be examined and the relative amount of each subject to be covered, you can choose suitable study materials. For beginning level jobs, or even advanced ones, if you have a pronounced weakness in some aspect of your training, read a modern, standard textbook in that field. Be sure it is up to date and has general coverage. Such books are normally available at your library, and the librarian will be glad to help you locate one. For entry-level positions, questions of appropriate difficulty are chosen – neither highly advanced questions, nor those too simple. Such questions require careful thought but not advanced training.

If the position for which you are applying is technical or advanced, you will read more advanced, specialized material. If you are already familiar with the basic principles of your field, elementary textbooks would waste your time. Concentrate on advanced textbooks and technical periodicals. Think through the concepts and review difficult problems in your field.

These are all general sources. You can get more ideas on your own initiative, following these leads. For example, training manuals and publications of the government agency which employs workers in your field can be useful, particularly for technical and professional positions. A letter or visit to the government department involved may result in more specific study suggestions, and certainly will provide you with a more definite idea of the exact nature of the position you are seeking.

III. KINDS OF TESTS

Tests are used for purposes other than measuring knowledge and ability to perform specified duties. For some positions, it is equally important to test ability to make adjustments to new situations or to profit from training. In others, basic mental abilities not dependent on information are essential. Questions which test these things may not appear as pertinent to the duties of the position as those which test for knowledge and information. Yet they are often highly important parts of a fair examination. For very general questions, it is almost impossible to help you direct your study efforts. What we can do is to point out some of the more common of these general abilities needed in public service positions and describe some typical questions.

1) General information

Broad, general information has been found useful for predicting job success in some kinds of work. This is tested in a variety of ways, from vocabulary lists to questions about current events. Basic background in some field of work, such as sociology or economics, may be sampled in a group of questions. Often these are principles which have become familiar to most persons through exposure rather than through formal training. It is difficult to advise you how to study for these questions; being alert to the world around you is our best suggestion.

2) Verbal ability

An example of an ability needed in many positions is verbal or language ability. Verbal ability is, in brief, the ability to use and understand words. Vocabulary and grammar tests are typical measures of this ability. Reading comprehension or paragraph interpretation questions are common in many kinds of civil service tests. You are given a paragraph of written material and asked to find its central meaning.

3) Numerical ability

Number skills can be tested by the familiar arithmetic problem, by checking paired lists of numbers to see which are alike and which are different, or by interpreting charts and graphs. In the latter test, a graph may be printed in the test booklet which you are asked to use as the basis for answering questions.

4) Observation

A popular test for law-enforcement positions is the observation test. A picture is shown to you for several minutes, then taken away. Questions about the picture test your ability to observe both details and larger elements.

5) Following directions

In many positions in the public service, the employee must be able to carry out written instructions dependably and accurately. You may be given a chart with several columns, each column listing a variety of information. The questions require you to carry out directions involving the information given in the chart.

6) Skills and aptitudes

Performance tests effectively measure some manual skills and aptitudes. When the skill is one in which you are trained, such as typing or shorthand, you can practice. These tests are often very much like those given in business school or high school courses. For many of the other skills and aptitudes, however, no short-time preparation can be made. Skills and abilities natural to you or that you have developed throughout your lifetime are being tested.

Many of the general questions just described provide all the data needed to answer the questions and ask you to use your reasoning ability to find the answers. Your best preparation for these tests, as well as for tests of facts and ideas, is to be at your physical and mental best. You, no doubt, have your own methods of getting into an exam-taking mood and keeping "in shape." The next section lists some ideas on this subject.

IV. KINDS OF QUESTIONS

Only rarely is the "essay" question, which you answer in narrative form, used in civil service tests. Civil service tests are usually of the short-answer type. Full instructions for answering these questions will be given to you at the examination. But in case this is your first experience with short-answer questions and separate answer sheets, here is what you need to know:

1) Multiple-choice Questions

Most popular of the short-answer questions is the "multiple choice" or "best answer" question. It can be used, for example, to test for factual knowledge, ability to solve problems or judgment in meeting situations found at work.

A multiple-choice question is normally one of three types—

- It can begin with an incomplete statement followed by several possible endings. You are to find the one ending which *best* completes the statement, although some of the others may not be entirely wrong.
- It can also be a complete statement in the form of a question which is answered by choosing one of the statements listed.
- It can be in the form of a problem – again you select the best answer.

Here is an example of a multiple-choice question with a discussion which should give you some clues as to the method for choosing the right answer:

When an employee has a complaint about his assignment, the action which will *best* help him overcome his difficulty is to
A. discuss his difficulty with his coworkers
B. take the problem to the head of the organization
C. take the problem to the person who gave him the assignment
D. say nothing to anyone about his complaint

In answering this question, you should study each of the choices to find which is best. Consider choice "A" – Certainly an employee may discuss his complaint with fellow employees, but no change or improvement can result, and the complaint remains unresolved. Choice "B" is a poor choice since the head of the organization probably does not know what assignment you have been given, and taking your problem to him is known as "going over the head" of the supervisor. The supervisor, or person who made the assignment, is the person who can clarify it or correct any injustice. Choice "C" is, therefore, correct. To say nothing, as in choice "D," is unwise. Supervisors have and interest in knowing the problems employees are facing, and the employee is seeking a solution to his problem.

2) True/False Questions

The "true/false" or "right/wrong" form of question is sometimes used. Here a complete statement is given. Your job is to decide whether the statement is right or wrong.

SAMPLE: A roaming cell-phone call to a nearby city costs less than a non-roaming call to a distant city.

This statement is wrong, or false, since roaming calls are more expensive.

This is not a complete list of all possible question forms, although most of the others are variations of these common types. You will always get complete directions for answering questions. Be sure you understand *how* to mark your answers – ask questions until you do.

V. RECORDING YOUR ANSWERS

Computer terminals are used more and more today for many different kinds of exams.

For an examination with very few applicants, you may be told to record your answers in the test booklet itself. Separate answer sheets are much more common. If this separate answer sheet is to be scored by machine – and this is often the case – it is highly important that you mark your answers correctly in order to get credit.

An electronic scoring machine is often used in civil service offices because of the speed with which papers can be scored. Machine-scored answer sheets must be marked with a pencil, which will be given to you. This pencil has a high graphite content which responds to the electronic scoring machine. As a matter of fact, stray dots may register as answers, so do not let your pencil rest on the answer sheet while you are pondering the correct answer. Also, if your pencil lead breaks or is otherwise defective, ask for another.

Since the answer sheet will be dropped in a slot in the scoring machine, be careful not to bend the corners or get the paper crumpled.

The answer sheet normally has five vertical columns of numbers, with 30 numbers to a column. These numbers correspond to the question numbers in your test booklet. After each number, going across the page are four or five pairs of dotted lines. These short dotted lines have small letters or numbers above them. The first two pairs may also have a "T" or "F" above the letters. This indicates that the first two pairs only are to be used if the questions are of the true-false type. If the questions are multiple choice, disregard the "T" and "F" and pay attention only to the small letters or numbers.

Answer your questions in the manner of the sample that follows:

32. The largest city in the United States is
    A. Washington, D.C.
    B. New York City
    C. Chicago
    D. Detroit
    E. San Francisco

1) Choose the answer you think is best. (New York City is the largest, so "B" is correct.)
2) Find the row of dotted lines numbered the same as the question you are answering. (Find row number 32)
3) Find the pair of dotted lines corresponding to the answer. (Find the pair of lines under the mark "B.")
4) Make a solid black mark between the dotted lines.

VI. BEFORE THE TEST

Common sense will help you find procedures to follow to get ready for an examination. Too many of us, however, overlook these sensible measures. Indeed, nervousness and fatigue have been found to be the most serious reasons why applicants fail to do their best on civil service tests. Here is a list of reminders:

- Begin your preparation early – Don't wait until the last minute to go scurrying around for books and materials or to find out what the position is all about.
- Prepare continuously – An hour a night for a week is better than an all-night cram session. This has been definitely established. What is more, a night a week for a month will return better dividends than crowding your study into a shorter period of time.
- Locate the place of the exam – You have been sent a notice telling you when and where to report for the examination. If the location is in a different town or otherwise unfamiliar to you, it would be well to inquire the best route and learn something about the building.
- Relax the night before the test – Allow your mind to rest. Do not study at all that night. Plan some mild recreation or diversion; then go to bed early and get a good night's sleep.
- Get up early enough to make a leisurely trip to the place for the test – This way unforeseen events, traffic snarls, unfamiliar buildings, etc. will not upset you.
- Dress comfortably – A written test is not a fashion show. You will be known by number and not by name, so wear something comfortable.
- Leave excess paraphernalia at home – Shopping bags and odd bundles will get in your way. You need bring only the items mentioned in the official notice you received; usually everything you need is provided. Do not bring reference books to the exam. They will only confuse those last minutes and be taken away from you when in the test room.
- Arrive somewhat ahead of time – If because of transportation schedules you must get there very early, bring a newspaper or magazine to take your mind off yourself while waiting.
- Locate the examination room – When you have found the proper room, you will be directed to the seat or part of the room where you will sit. Sometimes you are given a sheet of instructions to read while you are waiting. Do not fill out any forms until you are told to do so; just read them and be prepared.
- Relax and prepare to listen to the instructions
- If you have any physical problem that may keep you from doing your best, be sure to tell the test administrator. If you are sick or in poor health, you really cannot do your best on the exam. You can come back and take the test some other time.

VII. AT THE TEST

The day of the test is here and you have the test booklet in your hand. The temptation to get going is very strong. Caution! There is more to success than knowing the right answers. You must know how to identify your papers and understand variations in the type of short-answer question used in this particular examination. Follow these suggestions for maximum results from your efforts:

1) Cooperate with the monitor

The test administrator has a duty to create a situation in which you can be as much at ease as possible. He will give instructions, tell you when to begin, check to see that you are marking your answer sheet correctly, and so on. He is not there to guard you, although he will see that your competitors do not take unfair advantage. He wants to help you do your best.

2) Listen to all instructions

Don't jump the gun! Wait until you understand all directions. In most civil service tests you get more time than you need to answer the questions. So don't be in a hurry. Read each word of instructions until you clearly understand the meaning. Study the examples, listen to all announcements and follow directions. Ask questions if you do not understand what to do.

3) Identify your papers

Civil service exams are usually identified by number only. You will be assigned a number; you must not put your name on your test papers. Be sure to copy your number correctly. Since more than one exam may be given, copy your exact examination title.

4) Plan your time

Unless you are told that a test is a "speed" or "rate of work" test, speed itself is usually not important. Time enough to answer all the questions will be provided, but this does not mean that you have all day. An overall time limit has been set. Divide the total time (in minutes) by the number of questions to determine the approximate time you have for each question.

5) Do not linger over difficult questions

If you come across a difficult question, mark it with a paper clip (useful to have along) and come back to it when you have been through the booklet. One caution if you do this – be sure to skip a number on your answer sheet as well. Check often to be sure that you have not lost your place and that you are marking in the row numbered the same as the question you are answering.

6) Read the questions

Be sure you know what the question asks! Many capable people are unsuccessful because they failed to *read* the questions correctly.

7) Answer all questions

Unless you have been instructed that a penalty will be deducted for incorrect answers, it is better to guess than to omit a question.

8) Speed tests

It is often better NOT to guess on speed tests. It has been found that on timed tests people are tempted to spend the last few seconds before time is called in marking answers at random – without even reading them – in the hope of picking up a few extra points. To discourage this practice, the instructions may warn you that your score will be "corrected" for guessing. That is, a penalty will be applied. The incorrect answers will be deducted from the correct ones, or some other penalty formula will be used.

9) Review your answers

If you finish before time is called, go back to the questions you guessed or omitted to give them further thought. Review other answers if you have time.

10) Return your test materials

If you are ready to leave before others have finished or time is called, take ALL your materials to the monitor and leave quietly. Never take any test material with you. The monitor can discover whose papers are not complete, and taking a test booklet may be grounds for disqualification.

VIII. EXAMINATION TECHNIQUES

1) Read the general instructions carefully. These are usually printed on the first page of the exam booklet. As a rule, these instructions refer to the timing of the examination; the fact that you should not start work until the signal and must stop work at a signal, etc. If there are any *special* instructions, such as a choice of questions to be answered, make sure that you note this instruction carefully.

2) When you are ready to start work on the examination, that is as soon as the signal has been given, read the instructions to each question booklet, underline any key words or phrases, such as *least, best, outline, describe* and the like. In this way you will tend to answer as requested rather than discover on reviewing your paper that you *listed without describing*, that you selected the *worst* choice rather than the *best* choice, etc.

3) If the examination is of the objective or multiple-choice type – that is, each question will also give a series of possible answers: A, B, C or D, and you are called upon to select the best answer and write the letter next to that answer on your answer paper – it is advisable to start answering each question in turn. There may be anywhere from 50 to 100 such questions in the three or four hours allotted and you can see how much time would be taken if you read through all the questions before beginning to answer any. Furthermore, if you come across a question or group of questions which you know would be difficult to answer, it would undoubtedly affect your handling of all the other questions.

4) If the examination is of the essay type and contains but a few questions, it is a moot point as to whether you should read all the questions before starting to answer any one. Of course, if you are given a choice – say five out of seven and the like – then it is essential to read all the questions so you can eliminate the two that are most difficult. If, however, you are asked to answer all the questions, there may be danger in trying to answer the easiest one first because you may find that you will spend too much time on it. The best technique is to answer the first question, then proceed to the second, etc.

5) Time your answers. Before the exam begins, write down the time it started, then add the time allowed for the examination and write down the time it must be completed, then divide the time available somewhat as follows:

- If 3-1/2 hours are allowed, that would be 210 minutes. If you have 80 objective-type questions, that would be an average of 2-1/2 minutes per question. Allow yourself no more than 2 minutes per question, or a total of 160 minutes, which will permit about 50 minutes to review.
- If for the time allotment of 210 minutes there are 7 essay questions to answer, that would average about 30 minutes a question. Give yourself only 25 minutes per question so that you have about 35 minutes to review.

6) The most important instruction is to *read each question* and make sure you know what is wanted. The second most important instruction is to *time yourself properly* so that you answer every question. The third most important instruction is to *answer every question*. Guess if you have to but include something for each question. Remember that you will receive no credit for a blank and will probably receive some credit if you write something in answer to an essay question. If you guess a letter – say "B" for a multiple-choice question – you may have guessed right. If you leave a blank as an answer to a multiple-choice question, the examiners may respect your feelings but it will not add a point to your score. Some exams may penalize you for wrong answers, so in such cases *only*, you may not want to guess unless you have some basis for your answer.

7) Suggestions
   a. Objective-type questions
      1. Examine the question booklet for proper sequence of pages and questions
      2. Read all instructions carefully
      3. Skip any question which seems too difficult; return to it after all other questions have been answered
      4. Apportion your time properly; do not spend too much time on any single question or group of questions
      5. Note and underline key words – *all, most, fewest, least, best, worst, same, opposite,* etc.
      6. Pay particular attention to negatives
      7. Note unusual option, e.g., unduly long, short, complex, different or similar in content to the body of the question
      8. Observe the use of "hedging" words – *probably, may, most likely,* etc.
      9. Make sure that your answer is put next to the same number as the question
      10. Do not second-guess unless you have good reason to believe the second answer is definitely more correct
      11. Cross out original answer if you decide another answer is more accurate; do not erase until you are ready to hand your paper in
      12. Answer all questions; guess unless instructed otherwise
      13. Leave time for review

   b. Essay questions
      1. Read each question carefully
      2. Determine exactly what is wanted. Underline key words or phrases.
      3. Decide on outline or paragraph answer

4. Include many different points and elements unless asked to develop any one or two points or elements
5. Show impartiality by giving pros and cons unless directed to select one side only
6. Make and write down any assumptions you find necessary to answer the questions
7. Watch your English, grammar, punctuation and choice of words
8. Time your answers; don't crowd material

8) Answering the essay question

Most essay questions can be answered by framing the specific response around several key words or ideas. Here are a few such key words or ideas:

M's: manpower, materials, methods, money, management
P's: purpose, program, policy, plan, procedure, practice, problems, pitfalls, personnel, public relations
   a. Six basic steps in handling problems:
      1. Preliminary plan and background development
      2. Collect information, data and facts
      3. Analyze and interpret information, data and facts
      4. Analyze and develop solutions as well as make recommendations
      5. Prepare report and sell recommendations
      6. Install recommendations and follow up effectiveness

   b. Pitfalls to avoid
      1. *Taking things for granted* – A statement of the situation does not necessarily imply that each of the elements is necessarily true; for example, a complaint may be invalid and biased so that all that can be taken for granted is that a complaint has been registered
      2. *Considering only one side of a situation* – Wherever possible, indicate several alternatives and then point out the reasons you selected the best one
      3. *Failing to indicate follow up* – Whenever your answer indicates action on your part, make certain that you will take proper follow-up action to see how successful your recommendations, procedures or actions turn out to be
      4. *Taking too long in answering any single question* – Remember to time your answers properly

IX. AFTER THE TEST

Scoring procedures differ in detail among civil service jurisdictions although the general principles are the same. Whether the papers are hand-scored or graded by machine we have described, they are nearly always graded by number. That is, the person who marks the paper knows only the number – never the name – of the applicant. Not until all the papers have been graded will they be matched with names. If other tests, such as training and experience or oral interview ratings have been given, scores will be combined. Different parts of the examination usually have different weights. For example, the written test might count 60 percent of the final grade, and a rating of training and experience 40 percent. In many jurisdictions, veterans will have a certain number of points added to their grades.

After the final grade has been determined, the names are placed in grade order and an eligible list is established. There are various methods for resolving ties between those who get the same final grade – probably the most common is to place first the name of the person whose application was received first. Job offers are made from the eligible list in the order the names appear on it. You will be notified of your grade and your rank as soon as all these computations have been made. This will be done as rapidly as possible.

People who are found to meet the requirements in the announcement are called "eligibles." Their names are put on a list of eligible candidates. An eligible's chances of getting a job depend on how high he stands on this list and how fast agencies are filling jobs from the list.

When a job is to be filled from a list of eligibles, the agency asks for the names of people on the list of eligibles for that job. When the civil service commission receives this request, it sends to the agency the names of the three people highest on this list. Or, if the job to be filled has specialized requirements, the office sends the agency the names of the top three persons who meet these requirements from the general list.

The appointing officer makes a choice from among the three people whose names were sent to him. If the selected person accepts the appointment, the names of the others are put back on the list to be considered for future openings.

That is the rule in hiring from all kinds of eligible lists, whether they are for typist, carpenter, chemist, or something else. For every vacancy, the appointing officer has his choice of any one of the top three eligibles on the list. This explains why the person whose name is on top of the list sometimes does not get an appointment when some of the persons lower on the list do. If the appointing officer chooses the second or third eligible, the No. 1 eligible does not get a job at once, but stays on the list until he is appointed or the list is terminated.

X. HOW TO PASS THE INTERVIEW TEST

The examination for which you applied requires an oral interview test. You have already taken the written test and you are now being called for the interview test – the final part of the formal examination.

You may think that it is not possible to prepare for an interview test and that there are no procedures to follow during an interview. Our purpose is to point out some things you can do in advance that will help you and some good rules to follow and pitfalls to avoid while you are being interviewed.

What is an interview supposed to test?

The written examination is designed to test the technical knowledge and competence of the candidate; the oral is designed to evaluate intangible qualities, not readily measured otherwise, and to establish a list showing the relative fitness of each candidate – as measured against his competitors – for the position sought. Scoring is not on the basis of "right" and "wrong," but on a sliding scale of values ranging from "not passable" to "outstanding." As a matter of fact, it is possible to achieve a relatively low score without a single "incorrect" answer because of evident weakness in the qualities being measured.

Occasionally, an examination may consist entirely of an oral test – either an individual or a group oral. In such cases, information is sought concerning the technical knowledges and abilities of the candidate, since there has been no written examination for this purpose. More commonly, however, an oral test is used to supplement a written examination.

Who conducts interviews?

The composition of oral boards varies among different jurisdictions. In nearly all, a representative of the personnel department serves as chairman. One of the members of the board may be a representative of the department in which the candidate would work. In some cases, "outside experts" are used, and, frequently, a businessman or some other representative of the general public is asked to serve. Labor and management or other special groups may be represented. The aim is to secure the services of experts in the appropriate field.

However the board is composed, it is a good idea (and not at all improper or unethical) to ascertain in advance of the interview who the members are and what groups they represent. When you are introduced to them, you will have some idea of their backgrounds and interests, and at least you will not stutter and stammer over their names.

What should be done before the interview?

While knowledge about the board members is useful and takes some of the surprise element out of the interview, there is other preparation which is more substantive. It *is* possible to prepare for an oral interview – in several ways:

1) Keep a copy of your application and review it carefully before the interview

This may be the only document before the oral board, and the starting point of the interview. Know what education and experience you have listed there, and the sequence and dates of all of it. Sometimes the board will ask you to review the highlights of your experience for them; you should not have to hem and haw doing it.

2) Study the class specification and the examination announcement

Usually, the oral board has one or both of these to guide them. The qualities, characteristics or knowledges required by the position sought are stated in these documents. They offer valuable clues as to the nature of the oral interview. For example, if the job involves supervisory responsibilities, the announcement will usually indicate that knowledge of modern supervisory methods and the qualifications of the candidate as a supervisor will be tested. If so, you can expect such questions, frequently in the form of a hypothetical situation which you are expected to solve. NEVER go into an oral without knowledge of the duties and responsibilities of the job you seek.

3) Think through each qualification required

Try to visualize the kind of questions you would ask if you were a board member. How well could you answer them? Try especially to appraise your own knowledge and background in each area, *measured against the job sought*, and identify any areas in which you are weak. Be critical and realistic – do not flatter yourself.

4) Do some general reading in areas in which you feel you may be weak

For example, if the job involves supervision and your past experience has NOT, some general reading in supervisory methods and practices, particularly in the field of human relations, might be useful. Do NOT study agency procedures or detailed manuals. The oral board will be testing your understanding and capacity, not your memory.

5) Get a good night's sleep and watch your general health and mental attitude

You will want a clear head at the interview. Take care of a cold or any other minor ailment, and of course, no hangovers.

What should be done on the day of the interview?

Now comes the day of the interview itself. Give yourself plenty of time to get there. Plan to arrive somewhat ahead of the scheduled time, particularly if your appointment is in the fore part of the day. If a previous candidate fails to appear, the board might be ready for you a bit early. By early afternoon an oral board is almost invariably behind schedule if there are many candidates, and you may have to wait. Take along a book or magazine to read, or your application to review, but leave any extraneous material in the waiting room when you go in for your interview. In any event, relax and compose yourself.

The matter of dress is important. The board is forming impressions about you – from your experience, your manners, your attitude, and your appearance. Give your personal appearance careful attention. Dress your best, but not your flashiest. Choose conservative, appropriate clothing, and be sure it is immaculate. This is a business interview, and your appearance should indicate that you regard it as such. Besides, being well groomed and properly dressed will help boost your confidence.

Sooner or later, someone will call your name and escort you into the interview room. *This is it.* From here on you are on your own. It is too late for any more preparation. But remember, you asked for this opportunity to prove your fitness, and you are here because your request was granted.

What happens when you go in?

The usual sequence of events will be as follows: The clerk (who is often the board stenographer) will introduce you to the chairman of the oral board, who will introduce you to the other members of the board. Acknowledge the introductions before you sit down. Do not be surprised if you find a microphone facing you or a stenotypist sitting by. Oral interviews are usually recorded in the event of an appeal or other review.

Usually the chairman of the board will open the interview by reviewing the highlights of your education and work experience from your application – primarily for the benefit of the other members of the board, as well as to get the material into the record. Do not interrupt or comment unless there is an error or significant misinterpretation; if that is the case, do not hesitate. But do not quibble about insignificant matters. Also, he will usually ask you some question about your education, experience or your present job – partly to get you to start talking and to establish the interviewing "rapport." He may start the actual questioning, or turn it over to one of the other members. Frequently, each member undertakes the questioning on a particular area, one in which he is perhaps most competent, so you can expect each member to participate in the examination. Because time is limited, you may also expect some rather abrupt switches in the direction the questioning takes, so do not be upset by it. Normally, a board member will not pursue a single line of questioning unless he discovers a particular strength or weakness.

After each member has participated, the chairman will usually ask whether any member has any further questions, then will ask you if you have anything you wish to add. Unless you are expecting this question, it may floor you. Worse, it may start you off on an extended, extemporaneous speech. The board is not usually seeking more information. The question is principally to offer you a last opportunity to present further qualifications or to indicate that you have nothing to add. So, if you feel that a significant qualification or characteristic has been overlooked, it is proper to point it out in a sentence or so. Do not compliment the board on the thoroughness of their examination – they have been sketchy, and you know it. If you wish, merely say, "No thank you, I have nothing further to add." This is a point where you can "talk yourself out" of a good impression or fail to present an important bit of information. Remember, *you close the interview yourself.*

The chairman will then say, "That is all, Mr. _____, thank you." Do not be startled; the interview is over, and quicker than you think. Thank him, gather your belongings and take your leave. Save your sigh of relief for the other side of the door.

How to put your best foot forward

Throughout this entire process, you may feel that the board individually and collectively is trying to pierce your defenses, seek out your hidden weaknesses and embarrass and confuse you. Actually, this is not true. They are obliged to make an appraisal of your qualifications for the job you are seeking, and they want to see you in your best light. Remember, they must interview all candidates and a non-cooperative candidate may become a failure in spite of their best efforts to bring out his qualifications. Here are 15 suggestions that will help you:

1) Be natural – Keep your attitude confident, not cocky

If you are not confident that you can do the job, do not expect the board to be. Do not apologize for your weaknesses, try to bring out your strong points. The board is interested in a positive, not negative, presentation. Cockiness will antagonize any board member and make him wonder if you are covering up a weakness by a false show of strength.

2) Get comfortable, but don't lounge or sprawl

Sit erectly but not stiffly. A careless posture may lead the board to conclude that you are careless in other things, or at least that you are not impressed by the importance of the occasion. Either conclusion is natural, even if incorrect. Do not fuss with your clothing, a pencil or an ashtray. Your hands may occasionally be useful to emphasize a point; do not let them become a point of distraction.

3) Do not wisecrack or make small talk

This is a serious situation, and your attitude should show that you consider it as such. Further, the time of the board is limited – they do not want to waste it, and neither should you.

4) Do not exaggerate your experience or abilities

In the first place, from information in the application or other interviews and sources, the board may know more about you than you think. Secondly, you probably will not get away with it. An experienced board is rather adept at spotting such a situation, so do not take the chance.

5) If you know a board member, do not make a point of it, yet do not hide it

Certainly you are not fooling him, and probably not the other members of the board. Do not try to take advantage of your acquaintanceship – it will probably do you little good.

6) Do not dominate the interview

Let the board do that. They will give you the clues – do not assume that you have to do all the talking. Realize that the board has a number of questions to ask you, and do not try to take up all the interview time by showing off your extensive knowledge of the answer to the first one.

7) Be attentive

You only have 20 minutes or so, and you should keep your attention at its sharpest throughout. When a member is addressing a problem or question to you, give him your undivided attention. Address your reply principally to him, but do not exclude the other board members.

8) Do not interrupt

A board member may be stating a problem for you to analyze. He will ask you a question when the time comes. Let him state the problem, and wait for the question.

9) Make sure you understand the question

Do not try to answer until you are sure what the question is. If it is not clear, restate it in your own words or ask the board member to clarify it for you. However, do not haggle about minor elements.

10) Reply promptly but not hastily

A common entry on oral board rating sheets is "candidate responded readily," or "candidate hesitated in replies." Respond as promptly and quickly as you can, but do not jump to a hasty, ill-considered answer.

11) Do not be peremptory in your answers

A brief answer is proper – but do not fire your answer back. That is a losing game from your point of view. The board member can probably ask questions much faster than you can answer them.

12) Do not try to create the answer you think the board member wants

He is interested in what kind of mind you have and how it works – not in playing games. Furthermore, he can usually spot this practice and will actually grade you down on it.

13) Do not switch sides in your reply merely to agree with a board member

Frequently, a member will take a contrary position merely to draw you out and to see if you are willing and able to defend your point of view. Do not start a debate, yet do not surrender a good position. If a position is worth taking, it is worth defending.

14) Do not be afraid to admit an error in judgment if you are shown to be wrong

The board knows that you are forced to reply without any opportunity for careful consideration. Your answer may be demonstrably wrong. If so, admit it and get on with the interview.

15) Do not dwell at length on your present job

The opening question may relate to your present assignment. Answer the question but do not go into an extended discussion. You are being examined for a *new* job, not your present one. As a matter of fact, try to phrase ALL your answers in terms of the job for which you are being examined.

Basis of Rating

Probably you will forget most of these "do's" and "don'ts" when you walk into the oral interview room. Even remembering them all will not ensure you a passing grade. Perhaps you did not have the qualifications in the first place. But remembering them will help you to put your best foot forward, without treading on the toes of the board members.

Rumor and popular opinion to the contrary notwithstanding, an oral board wants you to make the best appearance possible. They know you are under pressure – but they also want to see how you respond to it as a guide to what your reaction would be under the pressures of the job you seek. They will be influenced by the degree of poise you display, the personal traits you show and the manner in which you respond.

ABOUT THIS BOOK

This book contains tests divided into Examination Sections. Go through each test, answering every question in the margin. At the end of each test look at the answer key and check your answers. On the ones you got wrong, look at the right answer choice and learn. Do not fill in the answers first. Do not memorize the questions and answers, but understand the answer and principles involved. On your test, the questions will likely be different from the samples. Questions are changed and new ones added. If you understand these past questions you should have success with any changes that arise. Tests may consist of several types of questions. We have additional books on each subject should more study be advisable or necessary for you. Finally, the more you study, the better prepared you will be. This book is intended to be the last thing you study before you walk into the examination room. Prior study of relevant texts is also recommended. NLC publishes some of these in our Fundamental Series. Knowledge and good sense are important factors in passing your exam. Good luck also helps. So now study this Passbook, absorb the material contained within and take that knowledge into the examination. Then do your best to pass that exam.

———

EXAMINATION SECTION

EXAMINATION SECTION
TEST 1

DIRECTIONS: Each question or incomplete statement is followed by several suggested answers or completions. Select the one that BEST answers the question or completes the statement. *PRINT THE LETTER OF THE CORRECT ANSWER IN THE SPACE AT THE RIGHT.*

1. If S, the subject that investigator H is tailing, enters a large department store, H should   1._____

    A. wait outside the store in a concealed place until S comes out
    B. follow S into the store
    C. enter the store, but wait by the door
    D. wait outside the store but in a position near the door S entered

2. Which of the following is MOST likely to indicate an attempt at falsification of a particular document?   2._____

    A. Change in style of handwriting within the document
    B. Illegible writing
    C. Erasures or alterations
    D. Folds or creases in the document

3. A subject being tailed during a foot surveillance quickly turns and confronts the shadower and states, *Say Bud, are you tailing me?*
Of the following, the MOST appropriate action for the shadower to take is to   3._____

    A. ignore the question and keep on walking
    B. admit that he is shadowing the subject but refuse to tell him why
    C. deny the accusation but give no explanations
    D. give some excuse for his presence in the form of a cover-up

4. K, an investigator, has been given the assignment of tailing S, a suspect, who will be traveling by car at night in the city.
Of the following, the SIMPLEST way for K to carry out this surveillance would be to   4._____

    A. mark S's car beforehand so it is identifiable at night
    B. memorize the model, color, and style of S's car
    C. memorize the license plate of S's car
    D. mechanically disable S's car so it will be unusable

5. The United States Treasury Department may prove to be a valuable source of information in specialized instances. Which of the following types of information usually would NOT be in the custody of that Federal agency?   5._____

    A. Immigration records
    B. Records of licensed manufacturers of narcotics
    C. Importers and exporters records
    D. Records of persons or firms manufacturing alcohol

6. Which of the following is a writ directing that documents or records be produced in court?   6._____

    A. Writ of habeas corpus   B. Subpoena habeas corpus
    C. Order, pro hoc vice   D. Subpoena duces tecum

7. *Modus Operands* is a phrase frequently used in investigative work to refer to a   7._____

    A. specific type of investigation
    B. particular policy in tracing missing persons
    C. manner in which a criminal operates
    D. series of crimes committed by more than one person

8. P, an investigator, has been assigned to interview W, a witness, concerning a minor auto-   8._____
mobile accident. Although P has made no breach of the basic rules of contact and
approach, he nevertheless recognizes that he and W have a personality clash and that a
natural animosity has resulted.
Of the following, P MOST appropriately should

    A. discuss the personality problem with W and attempt to resolve the difference
    B. stop the interview on some pretext and leave in a calm and pleasant manner,
       allowing an associate to continue the interview
    C. ignore the personality problem and continue as though nothing had happened
    D. change the subject matter being discussed since the facts sought may be the
       source of the animosity

9. Assume that an investigator desires to interview W, a reluctant witness to a bribery   9._____
attempt that took place several weeks previously. Assume further that the interview can
take place at a location to be designated by the interviewer.
Of the following, the place of interview should PREFERABLY be the

    A. office of the interviewer
    B. home of W
    C. office of W
    D. scene where the event took place

10. Assume that T, an investigator, is testifying in court. He does not clearly remember the   10._____
details of the incident about which he is testifying.
Of the following, the MOST appropriate action for T to take is to

    A. admit he does not remember the details and go on to the next question
    B. look at his statement previously given to the attorney interviewing him before trial
    C. refresh his memory by referring to his notebook
    D. testify to only those items he can recall

11. Assume that as an investigator you are interviewing W, a witness. During the interview, it   11._____
becomes apparent that W's statements are inaccurate and at variance with the facts previously established.
In these circumstances, it would be BEST for you to

    A. tell W that his statements are inaccurate and point out how they conflict with previ-
       ously established facts
    B. reword your questions and ask additional questions about the facts being dis-
       cussed
    C. warn W that he may be required to testify under oath at a later date
    D. ignore W's statements if you have other information that support the facts

12. Assume that W, a witness being interviewed by you, an investigator, shows a tendency   12.____
to ramble. His answers to your questions are lengthy and not responsive.
In this situation, the BEST action for you to take is to

    A. permit W to continue because at some point he will tell you the information sought
    B. tell W that he is rambling and unresponsive and that more will be accomplished if
he is brief and to the point
    C. control the interview so that complete and accurateinformation is obtained
    D. patiently listen to W since rambling is W's style and it cannot be changed

13. Assume that an investigator is to interview a witness. Of the following, the BEST proce-   13.____
dure for the investigator to follow in regard to the use of his notebook is to

    A. take out his notebook at the start of the interview and immediately begin taking
notes
    B. memorize the important facts related during the interview and enter them after the
interview has been completed
    C. advise the witness that all his answers are being taken down to insure that he will
tell the truth
    D. establish rapport with the witness and ask permission to jot down various data in
his notebook

14. The first duty of the investigator who has in his possession a document which may be   14.____
used in evidence is to preserve it in its original condition.
Following are three actions which might constitute rules for the handling of a document:
    I. Pick up the document with tweezers or a pin
    II. Staple the document to a folder so that it is protected
    III. Photograph or photocopy the document
Which one of the following choices MOST accurately classifies the above statements
into those which are APPROPRIATE and those which are NOT APPROPRIATE as
procedures for handling such documents?

    A. I and III are appropriate, but II is not appropriate.
    B. I and II are appropriate, but III is not appropriate.
    C. II is appropriate, but I and III are not appropriate.
    D. III is appropriate, but I and II are not appropriate.

15. Of the following, which one would be the CLEAREST indication that a suspicious check   15.____
is a forgery?

    A. There are smudges from carbon paper at the edges of the back of the check.
    B. The signature on the check is an exact duplicate of an authentic signature.
    C. The amount of the check has been crossed out and a new amount written in.
    D. Two different color inks were used in making out the check.

16. Assume an investigator is making an inspection of a desk and finds a writing pad on   16.____
which a suspect may have written. The top page of the pad has indentations which were
formed when the previous page was written on. Following are three procedures which
might be appropriate in order to read the indentation:

    I. Hold the paper in such a manner that a single light source falls along the sheet at a parallel or oblique angle.

   II. Soak the pad in water and thoroughly dry it in the sun.

  III. Rub a piece of carbon paper lightly across the underside of the paper in question.

Which one of the following choices classifies the above statements into those which are APPROPRIATE procedures and those which are NOT APPROPRIATE?

  A. I and II are appropriate, but III is not appropriate.
  B. II and III are appropriate, but I is not appropriate.
  C. I and III are appropriate, but II is not appropriate.
  D. II is appropriate, but I and III are not appropriate.

17. In order to conduct an effective interview, an interviewer's attention must be continuously directed in two ways, toward himself as well as toward the interviewee. Of the following, the PRIMARY danger in this division of attention is that the   17.____

  A. interviewer's behavior may become less natural and thus alienate the interviewee
  B. interviewee's span of attention will be shortened
  C. interviewer's response may be interpreted by the interviewee as being antagonistic
  D. interviewee's more or less concealed prejudices will come to the surface

18. X and Y go into a vault together and close the door. A shot is heard, and Y rushes out with a smoking gun in his hand.
A witness to his event who said *Y shot X* would be offering   18.____

  A. direct evidence   B. real evidence
  C. circumstantial evidence   D. hearsay evidence

19. Assume that an investigator is attempting to get a suspect to agree to take a lie detector or polygraph test.
Which of the following actions on the part of the investigator would be LEAST appropriate?   19.____

  A. Describe the test to the suspect in simple language so that he understands the procedure.
  B. Suggest that the test is a means for the suspect to indicate his innocence.
  C. Discuss the test's capability of indicating whether a person is telling the truth.
  D. Suggest that a refusal to take the test indicates guilt.

20. The term *corpus delicti* is MOST appropriately used to refer to   20.____

  A. a body of criminal law   B. the body of a person
  C. a body of civil law   D. the body of a crime

21. Which of the following is considered the BEST type of permanent ink to use in preparing documents?   21.____

  A. Ball point   B. Nigrosine
  C. Log wood   D. Iron gallotannate

22. An important aspect of investigative work is the preservation of materials which may be used as evidence. Following are three statements which might constitute rules for the proper handling of blood in a fluid condition found at a crime scene:

    I.   The blood should be removed with an eye dropper and placed in a test tube.

    II. Saline solution should be added to the blood sample in a ratio of 1 to 4.

    III. The sample blood should be frozen and delivered to the laboratory as soon as possible.

Which of the following choices classifies the above actions into those which are APPROPRIATE and those which are INAPPROPRIATE?

    A. I and II are appropriate, but III is inappropriate.
    B. I and III are appropriate, but II is inappropriate.
    C. I is appropriate, but II and III are inappropriate.
    D. III is appropriate, but I and II are inappropriate.

22.____

23. The term *entrapment* refers to the act of

    A. peace officers or agents of the government in inducing a person to commit a crime not contemplated by him for the purpose of instituting a criminal prosecution against him
    B. private individuals inducing a person to commit an act not contemplated by him for the purpose of bringing a civil action against him
    C. peace officers or agents of the government in observing a person engaged in the commission of a criminal act and, therefore, obtaining direct evidence against the person
    D. private individuals or investigators in interrupting a person engaged in committing a criminal act

23.____

24. Assume you are investigating a person who is alleged to be an officer in a manufacturing corporation doing business in New York City.
Which of the following sources of information is the LEAST appropriate source to consult in checking whether this is true?

    A. POOR'S REGISTER OF DIRECTORS AND EXECUTIVES
    B. POLK'S BANKER'S ENCYCLOPEDIA
    C. MOODY'S MANUAL OF INVESTMENTS, AMERICAN AND FOREIGN
    D. POLK'S COPARTNERSHIP AND CORPORATION DIRECTORY

24.____

25. If an investigator is assigned to the surveillance of a suspect which requires the use of an automobile, it would generally be LEAST advisable for him to use a car

    A. rented from a rental agency
    B. personally owned by the investigator
    C. bearing special unregistered plates
    D. borrowed by someone who is trustworthy but has no official associations

25.____

KEY (CORRECT ANSWERS)

1.	B		11.	B
2.	C		12.	C
3.	D		13.	D
4.	A		14.	A
5.	A		15.	B
6.	D		16.	C
7.	C		17.	A
8.	B		18.	C
9.	A		19.	D
10.	C		20.	D

21.	D
22.	A
23.	A
24.	B
25.	B

TEST 2

DIRECTIONS: Each question or incomplete statement is followed by several suggested answers or completions. Select the one that BEST answers the question or completes the statement. *PRINT THE LETTER OF THE CORRECT ANSWER IN THE SPACE AT THE RIGHT.*

1. Following are three statements regarding writing instruments: 1.____
    I. The hardness of the lead and the sharpness of the point affect the appearance of pencil writing.
    II. The ballpoint pen obscures the writer's ability to exhibit his characteristic habits of quality, rhythm, and shading.
    III. An examination of writing performed with a ballpoint pen easily reveals the angle at which the pen was held with relation to the writer's body and the paper.
   Which of the following choices classifies the above statements into those which are generally CORRECT and those which are generally INCORRECT?

    A. I is correct, but II and III are incorrect.
    B. II is correct, but I and III are incorrect.
    C. I and II are correct, but III is incorrect.
    D. I and III are correct, but II is incorrect.

2. Following are three statements regarding procedures to be followed in obtaining exemplars from a suspect which may or may not be appropriate: 2.____
    I. After the suspect is seated and provided with writing materials, the investigator should dictate the comparison text, always indicating punctuation and paragraphing.
    II. The material should be dictated several times, the speed of the dictation being increased each time so that the suspect will be inclined to lapse into his normal handwriting habits.
    III. As each sheet is completed, it should be removed from the suspect so that he will not be able to imitate the first exemplars he has prepared.
   Which of the following choices classifies the above procedures into those which are APPROPRIATE and those which are INAPPROPRIATE?

    A. I and II are appropriate, but III is inappropriate.
    B. I and III are appropriate, but II is inappropriate.
    C. I is appropriate, but II and III are inappropriate.
    D. III is appropriate, but I and II are inappropriate.

3. During an investigation, it may be necessary to take a *deposition*. 3.____
   The one of the following which BEST describes a *deposition* is

    A. a record made of the case progress
    B. a statement made by a witness in which he agrees to give testimony in court without resort to subpoena
    C. testimony of a witness reduced to writing under oath or affirmation, in answer to interrogatories
    D. another name for an *affidavit*

4. Examination of handwriting on the basis of comparing the outer shapes of letters is known as the _____ method.

    A. holographic
    B. penographic
    C. calligraphic
    D. pedographic

4.____

5. An investigator who receives a lead from an anonymous phone caller would generally be BEST advised to

    A. ignore the information as unfounded
    B. tell the informant to call back when he is ready to divulge his identity
    C. determine from the informant the motivation behind his making the call
    D. get all relevant information possible on the assumption he will not hear from the caller again

5.____

6. In order to demonstrate his findings to the court, a document examiner must use enlarged, mounted photographs. Which of the following should ALSO be submitted to the court?

    A. Color enlargements, as well as black and white
    B. Normal-size photographs of the enlarged documents
    C. Negatives of the enlarged photographs
    D. Duplicates of the enlarged photographs

6.____

7. X, an investigator, has come upon a few documents belonging to Y, a person whom X is investigating. The documents cannot be taken or moved.
Of the following, the MOST appropriate action for X to take is to

    A. make a record of the documents, making certain to include any names, addresses, and numbers mentioned even though they may appear meaningless at the time of discovery
    B. make a record only of those documents deemed relevant by him at the time of discovery, including names, addresses, and numbers mentioned
    C. leave the documents without making any notes because documents that cannot be moved may not be copied
    D. make a record only of those names, addresses, or numbers mentioned which are clearly relevant to the case

7.____

8. Assume that you are interviewing W, a neighbor of N, whom you are investigating. It is important to establish whether or not N uses alcoholic beverages excessively.
Which of the following questions is MOST appropriate for obtaining the information you seek?

    A. Have you ever seen N intoxicated?
    B. Can you tell me something about N's habits?
    C. Do you know whether or not N is a patron of nearby bars?
    D. What is N's reputation in the neighborhood?

8.____

9. A check may be altered to change the amount, the name, or some other element.
The one of the following which can BEST be used to discover any changes is

    A. a magnetometer
    B. an ultra-violet lamp
    C. a tensimeter
    D. polarography

9.____

10. Z, an investigator, is attempting to interview W concerning an accident witnessed by W. However, W is disinterested and indifferent.
In order to encourage W's cooperation, Z should

    A. stimulate W's interest by stressing the importance of the information that he possesses
    B. impress upon W that Z is an investigator performing an official function
    C. warn W that the withholding of information may be considered as an obstruction of justice
    D. gain W's sympathy for Z, who is merely trying to do his job

10.____

11. Of the following, the three types of ink MOST commonly used in the United States today are:

    A. gallotannic, logwood, and nigrosine
    B. gallotannic, vanadium, and wolfram
    C. wolfram, logwood, and nigrosine
    D. vanadium, logwood, and nigrosine

11.____

12. Which of the following BEST describes the science of poroscopy?
Identification

    A. by the casting of footprints
    B. by the tracing of tools used in a crime
    C. by means of sweat pores indicated on a fingerprint
    D. through the examination of human hairs

12.____

13. Which of the following statements concerning the folding of paper is generally ACCURATE?

    A. When uncut paper has been folded, the fibers remain unbroken.
    B. If an ink line is first drawn and the paper is subsequently folded, the line over the fold will not be even and uniform.
    C. If an ink line is written over an already existing fold, the ink will spread over the fold but protruding fibers will not become stained.
    D. It is almost impossible to determine whether a lead pencil line was drawn on a paper before or after it was folded.

13.____

14. All of the following are generally good methods of making erased lead-pencil writing visible EXCEPT

    A. examination in non-polarized light
    B. use of iodine fumes
    C. contrast photography
    D. photography in oblique light

14.____

15. Following are four statements concerning crime-scene photography that may or may not be valid:

    I. The general procedure of crime-scene photography aims at obtaining views of broad areas of the crime locale, supplemented by closer views of sections containing important detail.
    II. The crime scene should be first photographed in its original, undisturbed state.

15.____

III. Crime-scene photographs are of great value to the investigator because they accurately show the distances between objects.

IV. If a room is to be photographed, a set of at least four views will be required to show the room adequately.

Which of the following choices MOST accurately classifies the above into those which are VALID procedures and those which are NOT VALID?

A. I and II are valid, but III and IV are not valid.
B. I, II, and IV are valid, but III is not valid.
C. III and IV are valid, but I and II are not valid.
D. I, II, and III are valid, but IV is not valid.

16. Following are four statements concerning the erasing of ink which may or may not be valid:

    I. It may be difficult to detect an erasure made with an eradicator, especially after a considerable length of time has elapsed.

    II. When an erasure has been made with a knife or rubber, it is generally easy to detect the area involved, as it is translucent.

    III. The sulfocyanic acid method is inappropriate for the detection of residue of iron-containing inks.

    IV. Examination with ultra-violet rays should not be strongly relied upon because clever forgers have been known to wash away all residue of eradication with distilled water.

Which of the following choices MOST accurately classifies the above statements into those which are generally VALID and those which are NOT VALID?

A. I and II are generally valid, but III and IV are not generally valid.
B. IV is generally valid, but I, II, and III are not generally valid.
C. I, II, and IV are generally valid, but III is not generally valid.
D. III and IV are generally valid, but I and II are not generally valid.

16._____

17. Following are four statements concerning fingerprints which may or may not be true:

    I. Plastic fingerprints are found on such objects as a bar of soap or ball of melted wax.

    II. Visible fingerprints are left by fingers covered with a colored material such as blood or grease.

    III. The majority of latent fingerprints are relatively invisible and must be developed.

    IV. Dirty surfaces and absorbent materials readily bear prints.

Which of the following choices MOST accurately classifies the above statements into those which are TRUE and those which are NOT TRUE?

A. I and II are true; III and IV are not true.
B. I and III are true; II and IV are not true.
C. I, II, and III are true, and IV is not true.
D. I, II, and IV are true, and III is not true.

17._____

18. Of the following, the method of fingerprint classification MOST commonly used in the United States is the _____ system.

A. Henry   B. Vucetich   C. Bertillon   D. Pottecher

18._____

19. Of the following, the term *curtilage* is MOST appropriately used to refer to
    19.____
    A. the enclosed space of ground and buildings immediately surrounding a dwelling
    B. a surgical procedure used to induce an abortion
    C. the illegal detention of suspects by law enforcement personnel
    D. a legal action taken by a judge to curtail the irrelevant testimony of witnesses in court

20. Which of the following statements is MOST valid as a guide to investigators in their dealings with informants?
    20.____

    A. Whether they are agreeable or not, informants should be made available for questioning by other agencies since they may have good information in areas other than those which directly concern you.
    B. Many informants work out of revenge, while some others do it only for money. Therefore, you should evaluate the information they give you with regard to their motivation.
    C. Informants tend to use their connections with law enforcement agencies. From time to time, they must be put in their place by letting them know they are *stool pigeons*.
    D. To cultivate informants, it is a good practice to give them some money in advance so they will be assured of a reward when they have good information.

21. The more meager the evidence against a suspect, the later the suspect should be allowed to know of it.
    As a practical rule to guide the investigator during an interrogation, the advice contained in this statement is GENERALLY
    21.____

    A. *bad,* chiefly because suspects have a right to know the details of the offense being investigated
    B. *good,* chiefly because the interrogator will not look foolish due to his lack of information
    C. *bad,* chiefly because the investigator will be unable to develop the proper rapport with the suspect during the interrogation
    D. *good,* chiefly because the suspect, not sensing the direction of the interrogation, is more likely to reveal information

22. Following are three statements concerning fingerprinting which may or may not be valid:
    22.____
       I. The best paper for fingerprinting purposes has a rough surface which will absorb ink.
       II. The subject should roll his fingers on the paper from right to left exercising as much pressure as possible on the paper to make a print.
       III. Fingerprints taken with stamp-pad ink are not usually legible or permanent.
    Which of the following classifies the above statements into thos which are VALID and those which are NOT VALID?

    A. I is valid, but II and III are not valid.
    B. I and II are valid, but III is not valid.
    C. II is valid, but I and III are not valid.
    D. III is valid, but I and II are not valid.

23. All of the following statements concerning fingerprints are true EXCEPT: 23.____
   A. There are no two identical fingerprints
   B. Fingerprint patterns are not generally changed by illness
   C. A modern procedure called dactylmogrification has been developed to change the fingerprints of individuals relatively easily
   D. if the skin on the fingertips is wounded, the whole fingerprint pattern will reappear when the wound heals

24. Mechanical erasures on a document produce an abrasion of the paper. Assume that a   24.____
   forger makes an ink writing which crosses an area which has been previously erased. Following are three conditions which might result in the erased area from such an action:
       I. The ink line is brighter.
       II. The ink line is wider.
       III. The ink line tends to run or feather out sideways.
   Which one of the following choices MOST accurately classifies the above statements into those which would result from writing over the erased area and those which would not?

   A. I and II would result, but III would not result.
   B. I and III would result, but II would not result.
   C. II would result, but I and III would not result.
   D. II and III would result, but I would not result.

25. In the investigation of the periodic theft of equipment from stockrooms, the detection of   25.____
   the thieves is USUALLY accomplished by

   A. the use of strict inventory controls
   B. careful background investigation of applicants for the stockroom jobs
   C. issuing photo identification cards to all employees of the agency
   D. the use of intelligent surveillance

_____

KEY (CORRECT ANSWERS)

1.	C		11.	A
2.	D		12.	C
3.	C		13.	D
4.	C		14.	A
5.	D		15.	B
6.	B		16.	C
7.	A		17.	C
8.	A		18.	A
9.	B		19.	A
10.	A		20.	B

21.	D
22.	D
23.	C
24.	D
25.	D

EXAMINATION SECTION
TEST 1

DIRECTIONS: Each question or incomplete statement is followed by several suggested answers or completions. Select the one that BEST answers the question or completes the statement. *PRINT THE LETTER OF THE CORRECT ANSWER IN THE SPACE AT THE RIGHT.*

1. Assume that you are interviewing a witness who is telling a story crucial to your investigation. It is important that you get all the facts being related by this witness. In order to secure this vital information, the BEST of the following techniques is to

    A. quietly interrupt the witness's story and request him to speak with deliberation so that you can record his statement
    B. guide the witness during his recital so that all important points are validated
    C. confine your activities during the story to brief note-taking; and after the information has been secured, request a full written statement
    D. inform the witness that he must relate all the facts as truthfully and concisely as possible

1.____

2. The statement of any witness obtained by an investigator in an interview should GENERALLY be considered

    A. as a lead requiring substantiation by additional evidence
    B. accurate if the witness appears honest and is cooperative
    C. unreliable if the witness has been involved in similar investigations
    D. as a fact admissible under the rules of evidence

2.____

3. During an important interview, an investigator takes notes from time to time but very rarely looks at the subject being questioned.
Such action on the part of the investigator is

    A. *unacceptable,* chiefly because during the actual interview an investigator should pay more attention to the witness's manner of giving the information rather than to the content of his statement
    B. *acceptable,* chiefly because data should be recorded at the earliest opportunity and important data should be noted meticulously
    C. *unacceptable,* chiefly because it inhibits the person being interviewed and is not conducive to a give-and-take discussion
    D. *acceptable,* chiefly because focusing attention on note-taking and not on the person being interviewed creates an impression of professional objectivity

3.____

4. The BEST source with which to check the credit rating of a business you are investigating is

    A. the Better Business Bureau
    B. Standard and Poor's
    C. Dun and Bradstreet, Inc.
    D. the State Attorney General's Office

4.____

5. Since he must, in the course of his investigations, interview persons with various person- 5._____
alities and attitudes, an investigator should GENERALLY adopt a method of interviewing
that

    A. is uniformly applicable to all types so that discrepancies in the accounts of individ-
uals may be readily detected
    B. can be adjusted to the persons whom he interviews
    C. is based on the premise that most witnesses tend to be uncooperative
    D. requires the investigator to spend as little time as possible in questioning witnesses

6. An investigator finds that X, Y, and Z are eyewitnesses to an incident under investigation. 6._____
He interviews X, who gives him a complete and very detailed statement about the incident. X also informs the investigator that he has discussed the matter with Y and Z, and
that each of them completely agrees with him as to what had occurred.
Under these circumstances, it would be MOST appropriate for the investigator to

    A. interview Y and Z before assessing the value of the statements made by the three
witnesses
    B. interview Y and Z and accept their versions if they both disagree with the story
given by witness X
    C. interview either Y or Z and close the investigation if the statement of either witness
agrees with the story given by witness X
    D. close the investigation on the basis of his interview with witness X since there is no
reason to assume that Y and Z will tell a different story

7. Which one of the following is a legal requirement for the admissibility of evidence in a 7._____
legal proceeding?

    A. Weight   B. Sufficiency
    C. Competency   D. Recency

8. Of the following diagrams, which one represents the CORRECT utilization of the ABC 8._____
Method of Surveillance?
Note: S - identifies the suspect's position
       X - identifies the positions of investigators
       Arrow indicates direction in which suspect is moving

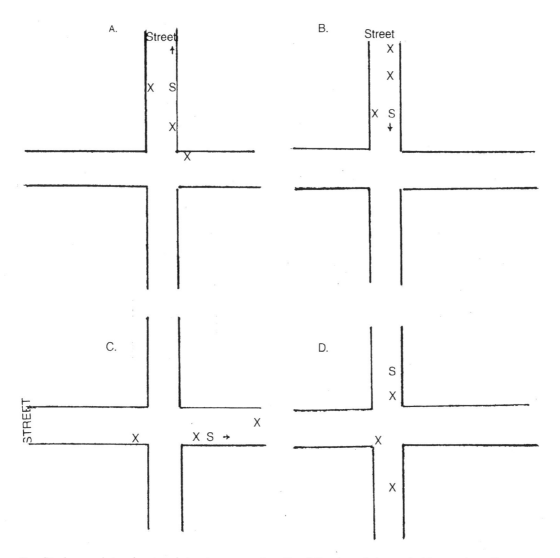

9. During an interview, an interviewee makes the following statement: *I have given the problem of getting a job a great deal of thought. I am looking primarily for an opportunity to grow and develop - to find the type of job that will provide the greatest challenge and bring out the best that is in me. Security probably ranks at the bottom of my list since I feel that I can always make a living somewhere.*
From an analysis of this statement, an investigator would be LEAST likely to conclude that the interviewee is

    A. capable of analytical thought
    B. looking for job satisfaction
    C. seeking self-improvement
    D. trying to cover for his lack of self-confidence

9.____

10. One of the more difficult tasks facing an investigator in an interview is to control the tendency of witnesses to ramble when giving information.
Of the following, the BEST technique for keeping a witness's comments pertinent is to

    A. ask questions which indicate the desired answer
    B. insist on *yes* and *no* answers to his questions
    C. construct questions that restrict the range of information which the witness can give in response
    D. ask precise questions so that the answers of the witness will necessarily be brief

10.____

11. The BASIC purpose of producing evidence in legal proceedings is to

    A. provide a permanent official record for legal action
    B. screen out confusing issues of law and fact
    C. determine the truth of a matter in issue
    D. insure that hearsay statements will be excluded

11.____

12. An investigator is handling a case involving an individual and finds that the case is proving very difficult because he has run out of leads to follow up.
Of the following, the BEST way for the investigator to deal with this case is FIRST to

    A. prepare a report of the case indicating that no further action can be taken
    B. place himself in the position of the person being investigated
    C. re-interview all those affected by the case until a new clue is revealed
    D. wait for the first break in the case which will give a substantial lead

12.____

13. Assume that you need to interview a person who is suspected of collaborating with the subject under investigation.
Of the following, the interviewing procedure that is MOST appropriate for handling this situation is to

    A. conduct a casual interview with the person on a pretext different from the actual purpose of the interview
    B. interview the person intensively by means of the *team* method until he breaks down and gives information
    C. insist that the suspected person cooperate
    D. plan to review every statement made by the person until he realizes that no fact will be overlooked

13.____

14. Assume that two disinterested individuals had directly witnessed the same event. An investigator who interviewed them received two distinctly different versions of this event. Which of the following assumptions PROBABLY accounts for the difference in the two versions?

    A. The event must have consisted of so many separate happenings that no one could understand everything that occurred.
    B. Each individual was selective in his perception of the event.
    C. The interviewing technique used by the investigator was instrumental in eliciting different facts from each individual.
    D. One of the individuals wishes to cooperate with the investigator, but the other did not.

14.____

15. During interviews, a certain investigator phrases follow-up questions mentally during   15.____
pauses while the subject is still answering the previous question.
This practice is GENERALLY

    A. *desirable,* chiefly because it gives the impression that the investigator is well-acquainted with all the facts
    B. *undesirable,* chiefly because the investigator cannot know whether such questions will be appropriate
    C. *desirable,* chiefly because it enables the investigator to pose new questions without significant breaks in the discussion
    D. *undesirable,* chiefly because it subjects the person being interviewed to a barrage of questions

16. Generally, a professional investigator's practice of training himself to give the impression   16.____
of telling the truth during court appearances is considered

    A. *desirable,* chiefly because only by such practice can he perfect his ability to give accurate testimony
    B. *undesirable,* chiefly because any deviation from the unadulterated truth by using a pretension constitutes perjury
    C. *desirable,* chiefly because such training lessens the possibility of his appearing nervous and timid while testifying, which might convey the impression that he is evasive or lying
    D. *undesirable,* chiefly because all testimony should be given in a natural manner, including hesitations, to avoid the court's suspicion that the witness has been coached

17. Assume that prior to an interview, a person makes a spontaneous declaration relating to   17.____
his case in the presence of an investigator.
According to a rule of evidence, the person's statement is GENERALLY

    A. *admissible,* only if the investigator testifies to the declaration and his testimony is corroborated by another person
    B. *inadmissible,* chiefly because it constitutes a hearsay declaration against the person's interest
    C. *admissible,* chiefly because it was not the product of the person's deliberation and reflection
    D. *inadmissible,* chiefly because the person was under duress when the exclamation was made

18. In order to break down the communication barriers between an interviewer and his sub-   18.____
ject, the interviewer should GENERALLY ask introductory questions which

    A. focus on the individual's job status
    B. can be answered in a *yes-or-no* fashion
    C. focus directly on official business
    D. are likely to be of mutual interest to the two parties

19. To introduce as evidence a set of business books prepared by a person other than the individual under investigation, preliminary evidence pertaining to the content of the books must first be established.
Which of the following does NOT constitute a fact which must be established before such books may be admitted as evidence?
The

    A. entries were made in the regular course of business at or about the time of the transactions involved
    B. books have been audited and certified as correct
    C. books are the regular books used for making business entries
    D. entries in the books were made by persons required to make them in the course of their regular duties

19.____

20. A person who is suffering from a mental disability is not necessarily disqualified from testifying as a witness in a legal proceeding PROVIDED that such person

    A. has the ability to recall and describe past events pertaining to the case
    B. is not an inmate of a mental institution
    C. is attended by a qualified psychiatrist at all times while in the courtroom
    D. swears that he knows the difference between right and wrong

20.____

21. Of the following public records, which is the BEST single source of information on the personal history and background of a subject?

    A. Birth or baptismal certificate
    B. Marriage license application
    C. Discharge certificate from the military services
    D. Income tax return

21.____

22. When it is necessary to prove the contents of a written instrument concerning a matter in dispute, the *best evidence rule* provides that

    A. the contents of written instruments must be subscribed and sworn to before a notary public to be admissible in legal proceedings
    B. no evidence outside the instrument itself shall be used to alter the wording of the instrument
    C. a witness who qualifies as an expert in handwriting identification shall first testify on the genuineness of the instrument
    D. the original instrument itself must be produced in court if it is available

22.____

23. Public documents, if otherwise competent, are admissible as evidence of the facts recorded therein, without the testimony of the officers who entered the facts, CHIEFLY because

    A. public records are subject to such strict security that the entries therein cannot be altered or falsified
    B. all such documents require further corroboration before they are admissible as proof of any facts recorded therein
    C. entries in these documents are made by officers who have sworn to perform their duties in the public interest
    D. hearsay evidence may not be admitted to prove a fact in dispute without the testimony of the officer who recorded it

23.____

24. One of the following ways in which an investigator might ordinarily detect an inconsistency in an interviewee's story is by   24.____

    A. having a third party present during the interview
    B. requesting the subject to speak more slowly
    C. observing the subject's manner of dress or attire
    D. watching the subject's facial expressions and mannerisms

25. The use of small talk or conversation about extraneous topics such as sports, the weather, or current events at the start of a routine interview designed to elicit information is GENERALLY considered   25.____

    A. *desirable,* chiefly because it gives the subject a chance to relax and relieve himself of the tension that normally develops before an interview
    B. *undesirable,* chiefly because it wastes the valuable time of subjects with matters that are unrelated to the purpose of the interview
    C. *desirable,* chiefly because it is the only way the interviewer is able to ascertain whether he and the subject will be able to develop rapport
    D. *undesirable,* chiefly because it is possible to obtain more information about the subject if he is unaware of the purpose of the interview

26. Assume that your superior assigns you to interview an individual who, he warns, seems to be highly *introverted.* You should be aware that, during an interview, such a person is likely to   26.____

    A. hold views which are highly controversial in nature
    B. be domineering and try to control the direction of the interview
    C. resist answering personal questions regarding his background
    D. give information which is largely fabricated

27. The one of the following persons who is MOST likely to be willing to give information leading to the apprehension of a suspect is someone who is   27.____

    A. friendly with the suspect
    B. afraid of the suspect
    C. interested in law enforcement
    D. seeking revenge against the suspect

28. During the course of a routine interview, the BEST tone of voice for an interviewer to use is   28.____

    A. authoritative   B. uncertain
    C. formal   D. conversational

29. It is recommended that interviews which inquire into the personal background of an individual should be held in private.
    The BEST reason for this practice is that privacy   29.____

    A. allows the individual to talk freely about the details of his background
    B. induces contemplative thought on the part of the interviewed individual
    C. prevents any interruptions by departmental personnel during the interview
    D. most closely resembles the atmosphere of the individual's personal life

30. Of the following, the MOST preferable way for an investigator to make a reference check   30.____
on a subject's previous employment in the area is to

    A. write to the employer and ask him to fill out a standard employee evaluation form
    B. call the employer and conduct a telephone interview
    C. write to the employer and request a personal interview
    D. telephone the employer and ask him to submit a written evaluation

31. Of the following, the BEST way for an investigator to prepare himself for a court appear-   31.____
ance as a witness is generally by

    A. memorizing every detail of the case in order to give an exact recital of the informa-
tion
    B. reviewing his notes and trying to fix in his mind the highlights of the case
    C. consulting with his superiors in order to ascertain which aspects of the case should
be emphasized
    D. studying all aspects of the case and writing out in detail the testimony he intends to
give under oath

32. When an investigator is called as a witness to relate a series of incidents, his testimony   32.____
should GENERALLY consist of

    A. a background narrative, followed by important facts and a concluding statement
    B. important facts, followed by a background narrative and a concluding statement
    C. details personally observed followed by any undeveloped leads
    D. a simple chronological account of the events he has observed

33. Of the following, an individual who smokes heavily during interrogation or an interview is   33.____
LEAST likely to experience a(n)

    A. decrease in mental efficiency
    B. decrease in physical efficiency
    C. state of high emotion during questioning
    D. emotional release during questioning

34. The BEST way for an investigator to handle a situation in which the person interviewed   34.____
asks a few slightly personal questions is generally to

    A. give quick, evasive answers and continue with the interview
    B. tell the person such questions are irrelevant and objectionable
    C. inquire fully into the person's reasons for wanting such information
    D. answer the questions briefly and truthfully

35. The CHIEF purpose of using surveillance in an investigation is to   35.____

    A. obtain information about persons and activities
    B. cause suspected persons to feel continuously uneasy
    C. maintain a close watch over hostile witnesses
    D. induce subjects to volunteer information

36. A *surreptitious* recording of an interview is one which is made 36.____

    A. whenever the information is highly technical
    B. to conceal the identity of the interviewee
    C. without the knowledge of the subject
    D. to encourage a subject to be more informative

37. All the means by which any alleged matter of fact, the truth of which is submitted to investigation, is established or disproved is the legal definition of 37.____

    A. proof
    B. burden of proof
    C. evidence
    D. admissibility of evidence

38. That section of an affidavit in which an officer empowered to administer an oath certifies that this document was *sworn to* before him is called a(n) 38.____

    A. affirmation
    B. jurat
    C. acknowledgement
    D. verification

39. In legal terminology, a *bailee* is a person who 39.____

    A. lawfully holds property belonging to another
    B. deposits cash or property for the release of an arrested person
    C. has been released from arrest on a bond that guarantees his court appearance
    D. deposits personal property as collateral for a debt

40. A specimen of handwriting of known authorship which can be used by an investigator for making a comparison with a questioned or suspected writing is called a(n) 40.____

    A. inscription
    B. precis
    C. coordinate
    D. exemplar

41. The attorney felt that his client would be *exonerated*. In this sentence, *exonerated* means MOST NEARLY 41.____

    A. unwilling to testify
    B. declared blameless
    C. severely punished
    D. placed on probation

42. The two witnesses were suspected of *collusion*.
In this sentence, the word *collusion* means MOST NEARLY 42.____

    A. a conflict of interest
    B. an unintentional error
    C. an illegal secret agreement
    D. financial irregularities

43. Many of the subject's answers during the interview were *redundant*.
In this sentence, *redundant* means MOST NEARLY 43.____

    A. uninformative
    B. thoughtful
    C. repetitious
    D. argumentative

44. He was assigned to investigate an individual who was *insolvent*.
In this sentence, *insolvent* means MOST NEARLY 44.____

    A. unable to pay debts
    B. extremely disrespectful
    C. difficult to understand
    D. frequently out of work

45. In his report, the investigator described several *covert* business transactions.   45._____
     In this sentence, *covert* means MOST NEARLY

    A. unauthorized   B. joint
    C. complicated   D. secret

KEY (CORRECT ANSWERS)

1. C	11. C	21. B	31. B	41. B
2. A	12. B	22. D	32. D	42. C
3. C	13. A	23. C	33. C	43. C
4. C	14. B	24. D	34. D	44. A
5. B	15. C	25. A	35. A	45. D
6. A	16. C	26. C	36. C	
7. C	17. C	27. D	37. C	
8. C	18. D	28. D	38. B	
9. D	19. B	29. A	39. A	
10. C	20. A	30. A	40. D	

TEST 2

DIRECTIONS: Each question or incomplete statement is followed by several suggested answers or completions. Select the one that BEST answers the question or completes the statement. *PRINT THE LETTER OF THE CORRECT ANSWER IN THE SPACE AT THE RIGHT.*

Questions 1-5.

DIRECTIONS: Questions 1 through 5 consist of two sentences which may or may not contain errors in word usage or sentence structure, punctuation, or capitalization. Consider a sentence correct although there may be other correct ways of expressing the same thought.
Mark your answer:
A. If only Sentence I is correct;
B. If only Sentence II is correct;
C. If Sentences I and II are both correct;
D. If Sentences I and II are both incorrect.

1. I. Being locked in his desk, the investigator felt sure that the records would be safe.   1.____
    II. The reason why the witness changed his statement was because he had been threatened.

2. I. The investigation had just began then an important witness disappeared.   2.____
    II. The check that had been missing was located and returned to its owner, Harry Morgan, a resident of Suffolk County, New York.

3. I. A supervisor will find that the establishment of standard procedures enables his staff to work more efficiently.   3.____
    II. An investigator hadn't ought to give any recommendations in his report if he is in doubt.

4. I. Neither the investigator nor his supervisor is ready to interview the witnesses.   4.____
    II. Interviewing has been and always will be an important asset in investigation.

5. I. One of the investigator's reports has been forwarded to the wrong person.   5.____
    II. The investigator stated that he was not familiar with those kind of cases.

Questions 6-8.

DIRECTIONS: Questions 6 through 8 are to be answered SOLELY on the basis of the following passage.

As investigators, we are more concerned with the utilitarian than the philosophical aspects of ethics and ethical standards, procedures, and conduct. As a working consideration, we might view ethics as the science of doing the right thing at the right time in the right manner in conformity with the normal, everyday standards imposed by society; and in conformity with the judgment society would be expected to make concerning the rightness or wrongness of what we have done.

An ethical code might be considered a basic set of rules and regulations to which we must conform in the performance of investigative duties. Ethical standards, procedures, and conduct might be considered the logical workings of our ethical code in its everyday application to our work. Ethics also necessarily involves morals and morality. We must eventually answer the self-imposed question of whether or not we have acted in the right way in conducting our investigative activities in their individual and total aspects.

6. Of the following, the MOST suitable title for the above passage is   6.____

     A. THE IMPORTANCE OF RULES FOR INVESTIGATORS
     B. THE BASIC PHILOSOPHY OF A LAWFUL SOCIETY
     C. SCIENTIFIC ASPECTS OF INVESTIGATIONS
     D. ETHICAL GUIDELINES FOR THE CONDUCT OF INVESTIGATIONS

7. According to the above passage, ethical considerations for investigators involve   7.____

     A. special standards that are different from those which apply to the rest of society
     B. practices and procedures which cannot be evaluated by others
     C. individual judgments by investigators of the appropriateness of their own actions
     D. regulations which are based primarily upon a philosophical approach

8. Of the following, the author's PRINCIPAL purpose in writing the above passage seems to have been to   8.____

     A. emphasize the importance of self-criticism in investigative activities
     B. explain the relationship that exists between ethics and investigative conduct
     C. reduce the amount of unethical conduct in the area of investigations
     D. seek recognition by his fellow investigators for his academic treatment of the subject matter

Questions 9-11.

DIRECTIONS: Questions 9 through 11 are to be answered SOLELY on the basis of the following passage.

The investigator must remember that acts of omission can be as effective as acts of commission in affecting the determination of disputed issues. Acts of omission, such as failure to obtain available information or failure to verify dubious information, manifest themselves in miscarriages of justice and erroneous adjudications. An incomplete investigation is an erroneous investigation because a conclusion predicated upon inadequate facts is based on quicksand.

When an investigator throws up his hands and admits defeat, the reason for this action does not necessarily lie in his possible laziness and ineptitude. It is more likely that the investigator has made his conclusions after exhausting only those avenues of investigation of which he is aware. He has exercised good faith in his belief that nothing else can be done.

This tendency must be overcome by all investigators if they are to operate at top efficiency. If no suggestion for new or additional action can be found in any authority, an investigator should use his own initiative to cope with a given situation. No investigator should ever hesitate to set precedents. It is far better in the final analysis to attempt difficult solutions, even if the chances of error are obviously present, than it is to take refuge in the spineless adage: If you don't do anything, you don't do it wrong.

9. Of the following, the MOST suitable title for the above passage is   9.____

    A. THE NEED FOR RESOURCEFULNESS IN INVESTIGATIONS
    B. PROCEDURES FOR COMPLETING AN INVESTIGATION
    C. THE DEVELOPMENT OF STANDARDS FOR INVESTIGATORS
    D. THE CAUSES OF INCOMPLETE INVESTIGATIONS

10. Of the following, the author of this passage considers that the LEAST important consid-   10.____
eration in developing new investigative methods is

    A. efficiency.   B. caution
    C. imagination   D. thoroughness

11. According to this passage, which of the following statements is INCORRECT?   11.____

    A. Lack of creativity may lead to erroneous investigations.
    B. Acts of omission are sometimes as harmful as acts of commission.
    C. Some investigators who give up on a case are lazy or inept.
    D. An investigator who gives up on a case is usually not acting in good faith.

Questions 12-15.

DIRECTIONS: Questions 12 through 15 are to be answered SOLELY on the basis of the following passage.

*Perpetrators of crimes are often described by witnesses or victims in terms of salient
facial features. The Bertillon System of Identification, which preceded the widespread use of
fingerprints,Was based on body measurements. Recently, there have been developments in
the quantification of procedures used in the classification and comparison of facial characteristics. Devices are now available which enable a trained operator, with the aid of a witness, to
form a composite picture of a suspect's face and to translate that composite into a numerical
code. Further developments in this area are possible, using computers to develop efficient
sequences of questions so that witnesses may quickly arrive at the proper description.*

*Recent studies of voice analysis and synthesis, originally motivated by problems of effi-
cient telephone transmission, have led to the development of the audio-frequency profile or
"voice print." Each voice print may be sufficiently unique to permit development of a classification system that will make possible positive identification of the source of a voice print. This
method of identification, using an expert to identify the voice patterns, has been introduced in
more than 40 cases by 15 different police departments. As with all identification systems that
rely on experts to perform the identification, controlled laboratory tests are needed to establish with care the relative frequency of errors of omission and commission made by experts.*

12. The MOST appropriate title for the above passage is   12.____

    A. TECHNOLOGY IN MODERN INVESTIGATIVE DETECTION
    B. IDENTIFICATION BY PHYSICAL FEATURES
    C. VERIFICATION OF IDENTIFICATIONS BY EXPERTS
    D. THE USE OF ELECTRONIC IDENTIFICATION TECHNIQUES

13. According to the above passage, computers may be used in conjunction with which of the following identification techniques?   13.____

    A. Fingerprints   B. Bertillon System
    C. Voice prints   D. Composite facial pictures

14. According to the above passage, the ability to identify individuals based on facial characteristics has improved as a result of   14.____

    A. an increase in the number of facial types which can be shown to witnesses
    B. information which is derived from other body measurements
    C. coded classification and comparison techniques
    D. greater reliance upon experts to make the identifications

15. According to the above passage, it is CORRECT to state that audio-frequency profiles or *voice prints*   15.____

    A. have been decisive in many prosecutions
    B. reduce the number of errors made by experts
    C. developed as a result of problems in telephonic communications
    D. are unlikely to result in positive identifications

Questions 16-20.

DIRECTIONS: Questions 16 through 20 are to be answered SOLELY on the basis of the following graph.

EMPLOYMENT APPLICATION INFORMATION
CHECKED BY INVESTIGATORS IN DEPARTMENT Z
CENTRAL CITY

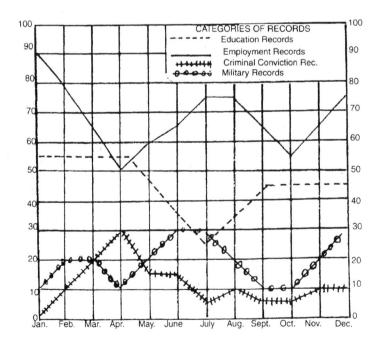

16. The category for which the SMALLEST number of record checks was made in _____ records.

    A. education   B. employment
    C. criminal conviction   D. military

16._____

17. In which of the following months did the combined number of criminal conviction record checks and military record checks EXCEED the number of education record checks?

    A. March   B. April   C. May   D. June

17._____

18. During which of the following months was the total number of records checked LARGEST?

    A. March   B. April
    C. September   D. November

18._____

19. Which of the following statements is INCORRECT according to the graph?

    A. Employment records checked each month always exceeded 45.
    B. Education records checked in February did not equal the number of education records checked in November.
    C. Military records checked per month increased from October to December.
    D. Criminal conviction records checked in any given month never exceeded the number of military records checked.

19._____

20. Of the total number of records checked in March, the percentage that were education records was MOST NEARLY

    A. 13%   B. 25%   C. 34%   D. 41%

20._____

Questions 21-25.

DIRECTIONS: Questions 21 through 25 are to be answered SOLELY on the basis of the information contained in the following tables.

STATUS OF TAX CASES ASSIGNED TO INVESTIGATORS, FISCAL YEAR, CENTRAL CITY, DEPARTMENT Y

Investigator	Cases Assigned	Cases Completed	Cases Pending at End of Fiscal Year
Albert	70	50	20
Bennett	90	60	30
Gordon	82	50	32
Nolton	70	40	30
Paxton	75	50	25
Rich	80	60	20

STATUS OF MISCELLANEOUS CASES ASSIGNED TO INVESTIGATORS FISCAL YEAR, CENTRAL CITY, DEPARTMENT Y

Investigator	Cases Assigned	Cases Completed	Cases Pending at End of Fiscal Year
Albert	25	20	5
Bennett	20	15	5
Gordon	18	13	5
Nolton	30	23	7
Paxton	17	17	0
Rich	32	24	6

21. Of the following, the investigator who completed the GREATEST percentage of his assigned tax cases in the fiscal year was

    A. Albert   B. Gordon   C. Paxton   D. Rich

21._____

22. The total number of the tax cases assigned in the fiscal year EXCEEDED the total number of miscellaneous cases assigned by

    A. 142   B. 325   C. 400   D. 467

22._____

23. Of the following, the two investigators who completed the SAME percentage of the miscellaneous cases assigned to them were

    A. Albert and Gordon
    C. Nolton and Paxton
    B. Gordon and Nolton
    D. Bennett and Rich

23._____

24. The average number of cases (both tax and miscellaneous) pending per investigator at the end of the fiscal year was MOST NEARLY

    A. 31   B. 28   C. 26   D. 5

24._____

25. Assume that the total number of miscellaneous cases pending at the end of the fiscal year is equal to 25% of the number of cases pending at the end of the previous fiscal year.
    What was the TOTAL number of miscellaneous cases pending at the end of the previous fiscal year?

    A. 28   B. 56   C. 74   D. 112

25._____

26. The head of an agency, in addressing a group of investigators, stated, *Whenever possible, do all you can to satisfy the needs of members of the public.*
    Which of the following is the LEAST acceptable procedure for investigators to use in implementing this policy?

    A. Handle public grievances and frustrations before they can accumulate.
    B. Satisfy public demands even though organizational goals may be compromised.
    C. Interpret rules and regulations reasonably.
    D. Use mass media to enlist support of programs to win public cooperation.

26._____

27. Of the following, the MOST important purpose of having a citizen advisory committee in a public agency is to   27.____

    A. make both the citizen groups and the public agency more responsive to the total public interest
    B. prevent fraud and mismanagement within the administration of the agency
    C. improve efficiency and encourage greater diligence on the part of agency personnel
    D. prevent the spread of unfavorable publicity about the agency's activities

28. Of the following, the term *public relations* in its application to any public agency is BEST defined as   28.____

    A. all the publicity received by the agency
    B. all the direct and indirect contacts between the agency itself and the clientele it deals with
    C. the sum total of efforts which the agency directs toward performing its functions
    D. de-emphasis of the agency's basic obligations which are not popular with its clientele

29. Assume that you receive a phone call from a man who refuses to identify himself and insists that he *knows for a fact* that an investigator on the staff of your agency has destroyed incriminating records upon receipt of a bribe.
The MOST appropriate action for you to take would be to   29.____

    A. refuse to discuss the matter unless the caller gives you his name and additional identification
    B. ask the caller for the facts and the name of the suspected investigator
    C. advise the caller that such a serious charge should be reported immediately to the police department
    D. politely advise the caller to report the facts in a letter to your agency head

30. In a public agency, the FIRST step in adopting a system which will give citizens an opportunity to make complaints against the agency's staff members is to   30.____

    A. establish an adequate complaint procedure
    B. design a citizen complaint report form
    C. establish physical facilities where complaints to the agency may be received
    D. initiate a public relations campaign informing the public that they may file complaints

31. Which of the following kinds of information is NOT found in the Official Directory of the City (Green Book)?   31.____

    A. The number of persons employed in each city agency
    B. A listing of police station houses and fire engine companies in each borough
    C. The names and addresses of all public high schools and city hospitals in each borough
    D. The names and addresses of federal, state, and city courts located within the city

32. An investigator should contact the State Department of Health to obtain information about persons who are licensed or qualified to practice as   32.____

    A. x-ray technicians   B. physiotherapists
    C. chiropractors   D. pharmacists

33. An employee complains that the city has refused to pay him some back salary for services he performed last year. This employee may bring legal action in the Small Claims Part if the amount of his claim does NOT exceed   33.____

    A. $1,000   B. $1,500   C. $300   D. $100

34. Experienced investigators have found that using the question-and-answer method in interviewing a witness, instead of allowing the witness to tell his own story freely and without interruption, MOST often tends to _____ the accuracy of the information given by the witness.   34.____

    A. *increase* both the scope and
    B. *increase* the scope but *decrease*
    C. *decrease* both the scope and
    D. *decrease* the scope but *increase*

35. Of the following, the STRONGEST indication that the signature on an important document is a forgery is that the suspected signature   35.____

    A. is partly illegible
    B. shows a noticeable trembling in certain letters
    C. shows that the writer retouched several letters
    D. is identical in all respects with a signature known to be genuine

36. Prior to writing the complete and final report at the conclusion of an important case, some investigators prepare an outline or blueprint of the investigative data compiled. All of the following are important advantages of preparing such an outline or blueprint EXCEPT that it   36.____

    A. results in the omission of less important or minor facts
    B. helps in achieving logical arrangement of the materials
    C. lessens chances of omitting essential facts
    D. aids in recognizing irrelevant details

37. In determining the validity of a document, the use of oblique lighting renders certain kinds of alterations visible.
Which of the following alterations would NOT be exposed by use of the oblique lighting technique?   37.____

    A. Abrasions and erasures made in order to change some significant part of a document
    B. Rubber-stamp impressions intended to validate a document but made from a non-genuine stamp
    C. Tears, mutilations, or excessive foldings made deliberately in order to conceal or obscure some damaging feature of the document
    D. Traced writing or writing taken from some pattern or model of genuine writing

38. When an investigator takes the witness stand for the prosecution, he must realize that the opposing counsel will GENERALLY endeavor to portray him as a(n)

    A. individual whose moral character is questionable and whose veracity therefore should be doubted
    B. disinterested collector and retailer of facts
    C. interested party who is trying to convict his client on the basis of insufficient evidence
    D. unprejudiced official with competent professional experience

38.____

39. Assume that on a certain day, an investigator finds that he has an excessive number of appointments for interviews and believes that he will be unable to keep them all during the course of the day.
    Of the following, the BEST action he could take is to

    A. ask a fellow investigator to help him conduct a group interview
    B. interview the maximum number that can be interviewed properly and reschedule the others for a future date
    C. proceed according to the established schedule
    D. shorten the length of time spent interviewing each person in order to insure that everyone is interviewed

39.____

40. There has been a tendency in recent times to publicize the use of instrumentation such as lie detectors, electronic eavesdropping devices, special cameras, and other technical devices in civil and criminal investigations. Of the following statements, the one which expresses a MAJOR weakness which results from relying too much on instrumentation as an investigative aid is:

    A. The use of these technical devices invariably violates the constitutional rights of persons subject to investigations
    B. Excessive publicity in the mass media about the success of these mechanical devices in solving difficult cases destroys their value as investigative aids
    C. These technical devices have a very limited value in cases where abundant physical evidence is available
    D. Inexperienced investigators are prone to place their faith in technical methods to the neglect of the more basic investigative procedures

40.____

KEY (CORRECT ANSWERS)

1.	D	11.	D	21.	D	31.	A
2.	B	12.	B	22.	B	32.	A
3.	A	13.	D	23.	D	33.	B
4.	C	14.	C	24.	A	34.	B
5.	A	15.	C	25.	D	35.	D
6.	D	16.	C	26.	B	36.	A
7.	C	17.	D	27.	A	37.	B
8.	B	18.	A	28.	B	38.	C
9.	A	19.	D	29.	B	39.	B
10.	B	20.	C	30.	A	40.	D

EXAMINATION SECTION
TEST 1

DIRECTIONS: Each question or incomplete statement is followed by several suggested answers or completions. Select the one that BEST answers the question or completes the statement. *PRINT THE LETTER OF THE CORRECT ANSWER IN THE SPACE AT THE RIGHT.*

1. Which of the following statements concerning the questioning of a witness by an investigator is VALID?   1.____

   A. The investigator should insist on *yes* and *no* answers from a witness because such responses insure accurate answers.
   B. The investigator should ask questions which suggest answers in order to speed the flow of information from the witness.
   C. Long and complicated questions should be used to impress the witness with the perceptiveness and intelligence of the investigator, thus insuring the cooperation of the witness.
   D. The investigator may be able to distinguish between honest mistakes and intended misrepresentations made by a witness by rewording his queries and by asking additional questions.

2. Following are three statements concerning interviewing and investigative practice: 2.____
   I. In order to improve his ability to interview persons successfully, the investigator should evaluate his performance during and after each interview
   II. An investigator who has detected evasiveness in the statements of a subject should write off these remarks as of little value to his investigation, and need not attempt to substantiate them
   III. In order to gain a psychological advantage over a difficult witness in an interview, it would be good practice for an investigator to ask the subject to sit in a chair other than the one the subject has selected

   Which of the following CORRECTLY classifies the above statements into those which are correct and those which are not?

   A. III is correct, but I and II are not.
   B. I is correct, but II and III are not.
   C. I and III are correct, but II is not.
   D. II and III are correct, but I is not.

3. An investigator, following a subject under surveillance, boards the same bus that the subject has just entered. If the subject suddenly jumps off before it starts, the investigator should   3.____

   A. stay on the bus, get off at the next stop, and wait for the next bus
   B. attempt to get off the bus before it starts
   C. stay on the bus, get off the next stop, and take another bus or taxi back to the original stop
   D. assume that he has been spotted and discontinue any further attempts to follow the subject

4. The technique of taking a written statement of the information the investigator obtains from a witness and then having the witness sign the statement is   4.____

A. *useful,* because a written statement presented to the court is more acceptable than oral testimony from that witness
B. *not useful,* because the witness will be intimidated
C. *useful,* because the witness may forget or change his version of what happened at a later time
D. *not useful,* because it delays the investigator's handling of the case

5. For evidence to be admissible in court, it must be   5._____

A. relevant but not necessarily material
B. material and relevant
C. of sufficient weight to influence any judicial decision or determination
D. of sufficient weight to be material

6. Which of the following statements BEST describes the term *judicial notice?*   6._____
The

A. act by which a court recognizes the truth of certain facts without the formal presentation of evidence
B. method by which a court notifies an individual that he is indicted
C. process by which notice of court action is given to the general public
D. communication of notice of court action, orally or in writing, directly to the affected person or the party to be charged

7. Assume that you are a supervising investigator interviewing a witness to alleged   7._____
employee corruption. In replying to a question on bribe-taking, the subject shifts to a totally unrelated topic.
Of the following, the BEST way to determine why the witness seems to be evading the question is to pursue the questioning

A. *aggressively,* chiefly because the subject is probably an unwilling accomplice to misconduct
B. *aggressively,* chiefly because the subject is probably protecting a fellow employee
C. *tactfully,* chiefly because the subject is probably unaware of any wrongdoing
D. *tactfully,* chiefly because the subject is probably withholding information that embarrasses him

8. An investigator usually develops positive or negative rapport with individuals he inter-   8._____
views.
When this occurs, the investigator should

A. control the nature and intensity of the relationship
B. direct his total attention to finishing the interview
C. develop a passive, professional attitude toward the interviewee
D. appear personally friendly to eliminate any negative feelings the interviewee may have

9. Which of the following techniques is MOST effective in detecting erasures on a document?   9._____
ment?

A. Look for an abrupt change in the style of writing
B. Examine the spacing of letters to see whether there has been crowding

C. Hold the document approximately edgewise to a light, close to the edge of the light's shade, and look for damaged paper fibers

D. Fume the document with the chemical vapors of gallo-tannate or nigrosine acid, which react with ink's residue

10. At times, an investigator may ask a subject for samples of his handwriting for purposes of comparison with a questioned document.
When taking such samples, which of the following procedures should be AVOIDED?

10._____

A. Placing the subject in a quiet place under minimal acceptable observation
B. Having the subject write something other than a list of signatures
C. Having the subject copy written or printed material
D. Removing each sample before the next one is started

11. Which of the following can PROPERLY be classified as *secondary* evidence?

11._____

A. Altered time sheets of accused employees
B. Eyewitness testimony regarding time and leave abuses
C. Official payroll roster records
D. Photocopies of forged checks

12. Following are three statements describing possible characteristics of fraudulent checks:

12._____

I. The first endorsement is clearly signed, matches the payee's name on the front, and appears right above the second endorsement
II. The name of the bank on which the check is drawn and its location are abbreviated on the face of the check
III. The digit and written amount of the check correspond exactly, and the payer's account number is inked over

Which of the following CORRECTLY classifies the above statements into those that describe characteristics generally peculiar to fraudulent checks and those that do not?

A. I and II are characteristic, but III is not.
B. I is a characteristic, but II and III are not.
C. II and III are characteristic, but I is not.
D. III is a characteristic, but I and II are not.

13. Following are four statements concerning communication between an investigator and an informant:

13._____

I. Meetings between an investigator and an informant should be held at the investigator's office
II. The proper name of the informant should not be used when telephoning
III. The investigator's organization should not be identified in any correspondence with the informant
IV. The circumstances surrounding meetings between the investigator and an informant should be repeated to establish a pattern

Which one of the following choices CORRECTLY classifies the above statements into those which are valid and those which are not valid as procedures for handling communications with an informant?

A. I and II are valid, but III and IV are not valid.
B. II and III are valid, but I and IV are not valid.
C. III is valid, but I, II, and IV are not valid.
D. IV is valid, but I, II, and III are not valid.

14. Of the following, the IMMEDIATE objective of an investigator, while speaking on the telephone to an anonymous person who is voluntarily offering information, should be to

    A. form an estimate of the informant's reliability
    B. decide on the motives and interests of the informer
    C. draw out all relevant information before the informer hangs up
    D. compare this information with that obtained from other sources

14._____

15. Supervising investigators are often called upon to provide subordinate investigators with on-the-job training. Following are three statements concerning the administration of on-the-job training:
    I. The supervisor selected to provide training must be an outstanding performer of the job he is teaching.
    II. The supervisor should have access to information about the training needs of the investigators he is to train.
    III. The subordinate investigators should be assigned to the work stations in which they will ultimately be employed.
Which of the following CORRECTLY classifies the above statements into those that are appropriate practices and those that are not?

    A. I is appropriate, but II and III are not.
    B. III is appropriate, but I and II are not.
    C. I and III are appropriate, but II is not.
    D. II and III are appropriate, but I is not.

15._____

16. Assume you are training a group of new investigators and that one member of the group is a slower learner than the others.
Of the following, the BEST way to handle this situation is to

    A. adapt your instruction speed to the rate of the slowest learner in order to reduce the possibility of frustrating him
    B. instruct at the level that is best suited to the majority of the group and give the slow learner individual help after the regular training sessions
    C. teach at the level at which you are most comfortable and handle problems as you become aware of them
    D. adjust your instruction speed to that of the slowest learner and provide him with extra remedial exercises or practice work

16._____

17. The one of the following that is a DISADVANTAGE of the conference approach to training investigators is that

    A. each investigator's ideas are critically evaluated by the other group members
    B. the informal atmosphere prevents the development of close relationships among investigators
    C. group members have time to reflect only on their own contributions and not on those of other investigators
    D. many investigators lack the skills or discipline to benefit from such training

17._____

18. Standard methods for performing various investigative tasks are useful MAINLY because they   18._____

    A. permit the supervisor to reduce the total time he spends on planning
    B. eliminate the need for monitoring costs
    C. enable the supervisor to spend less time on routine and detail
    D. reduce the number of forms needed to complete the tasks

19. Assume that, in one agency, the average number of absences per employee varies greatly from one investigative unit to another but the physical working conditions and type of work performed are similar in each of these units.   19._____
Of the following, the MOST probable cause of the differences in the amount of absenteeism is the

    A. educational background of the employees
    B. number of female employees in the agency
    C. attitudes of the supervisors
    D. existence of an agency medical unit

20. In order to learn their job properly, newly hired investigators must receive an indication from their supervisors of the quality of their performance. The one of the following techniques that provides the MOST constructive *feedback* from supervisors to their subordinates is   20._____

    A. praising all aspects of subordinates' performance
    B. pointing out to subordinates that mistakes may result in poor probationary reports
    C. drawing the subordinates' attention to how close their performance is to the expected level of performance
    D. preparing written critiques for study by subordinates

21. Of the following, the BEST way for a supervisor to reduce absenteeism within his unit is to   21._____

    A. inform subordinates that all excuses due to illness will be referred to the personnel officer
    B. discuss with individual employees the reasons for their absences
    C. assign less desirable work to those absent most often
    D. recommend that employees who are absent most often be transferred to other units

22. Of the following, the MOST important factor in determining whether a supervisor is a success or a failure as a manager is his ability to   22._____

    A. do all work assigned to his unit better than his subordinates can
    B. make suggestions which are acceptable to top management
    C. train employees for various responsibilities
    D. delegate work so that it is performed effectively

Questions 23-25.

DIRECTIONS: Below is a report consisting of 15 numbered sentences, some of which are not consistent with the principles of good report writing. Answer Questions 23 through 25 SOLELY on the basis of the information contained in the report and your knowledge of investigative principles and practices.

To: Tom Smith, Administrative Investigator
From: John Jones, Supervising Investigator

1. On January 7, I received a call from Mrs. H. Harris of 684 Sunset Street, Brooklyn.
2. Mrs. Harris informed me that she wanted to report an instance of fraud relating to public assistance payments being received by her neighbor, Mrs. I Wallace.
3. I advised her that such a subject would best be discussed in person.
4. I then arranged a field visitation for January 10 at Mrs. Harris' apartment, 684 Sunset Street, Brooklyn.
5. On January 10, I discussed the basis for Mrs. Harris' charge against Mrs. Wallace at the former's apartment.
6. She stated that her neighbor is receiving Aid to Dependent Children payments for seven children, but that only three of her children are still living with her.
7. In addition, Mrs. Harris also claimed that her husband, whom she reported to the authorities as missing, usually sees her several times a week.
8. After further questioning, Mrs. Harris admitted to me that she had been quite friendly with Mrs. Wallace until they recently argued about trash left in their adjoining hall corridor.
9. However, she firmly stated that her allegations against Mrs. Wallace were valid and that she feared repercussions for her actions.
10. At the completion of the interview, I assured Mrs. Harris of the confidentiality of her statements and that an attempt would be made to verify her allegations.
11. As I was leaving Mrs. Harris' apartment, I noticed a man, aged approximately 45, walking out of Mrs. Wallace's apartment.
12. I followed him until he entered a late model green Oldsmobile and sped away.
13. On January 3, I returned to 684 Sunset Court, having determined that Mrs. Wallace is receiving assistance as indicated by Mrs. Harris.
14. However, upon presentation of official identification Mrs. Wallace refused to admit me to her apartment or grant an interview.
15. I an therefore referring this matter to you for further instructions.

John Jones
Supervising Investigator

23. The one of the following statements that clearly lacks vital information is statement   23._____

    A. 8   B. 10   C. 12   D. 14

24. Which of the following sentences from the report is ambiguous? Sentence   24._____

    A. 2   B. 3   C. 7   D. 10

25. Which of the following sentences contains information contradicting other data in the above report? Sentence   25._____

    A. 3   B. 8   C. 10   D. 13

KEY (CORRECT ANSWERS)

1.	D	11.	D
2.	C	12.	C
3.	A	13.	B
4.	C	14.	C
5.	B	15.	D
6.	A	16.	B
7.	D	17.	D
8.	A	18.	C
9.	C	19.	C
10.	C	20.	C

21.	B
22.	D
23.	C
24.	C
25.	D

EXAMINATION SECTION
TEST 1

DIRECTIONS: Each question or incomplete statement is followed by several suggested answers or completions. Select the one that BEST answers the question or completes the statement. *PRINT THE LETTER OF THE CORRECT ANSWER IN THE SPACE AT THE RIGHT.*

1. During an interview with a witness, the investigator should carefully observe the witness's gestures and facial expressions.
   To interpret the meaning of these actions, the investigator should do all of the following EXCEPT to

   A. try to *read* the situation in which a puzzling gesture is used
   B. ask questions that relate specifically to the gesture
   C. take an educated guess based on past experience
   D. rely on the standard meaning of the gesture

   1.____

2. Of the following, the MOST important skill for a supervisor of investigators to possess is the ability to

   A. communicate effectively
   B. obtain the respect of his staff
   C. remain calm in pressure situations
   D. develop high morale among his subordinates

   2.____

3. Following are three statements concerning the preparation by an investigator of a written statement taken from a witness:
   I. Have each page initialed by the witness
   II. Correct and initial any mistakes in grammar that are made by the witness
   III. Leave space between paragraphs to facilitate the addition of notes and comments.
   Which of the following correctly classifies the above statements into those that are valid and those that are not?

   A. I is valid, but II and III are not.
   B. II and III are valid, but I is not.
   C. III is valid, but I and II are not.
   D. I and II are valid, but III is not.

   3.____

4. Assume, as an investigator, you are questioning an employee of your agency suspected of misstating previous work experience on his employment application. You notice that the employee is reluctant to admit that his previous statements were inaccurate.
   The one of the following that is the BEST method of obtaining the truth from this employee would be for you to

   A. tell him that his job is not in jeopardy
   B. make him feel he is not being criticized
   C. have him discuss the matter with your supervisor
   D. allow him to correct any inaccuracies on his employment application

   4.____

5. If several witnesses describing the same occurrence agree on most details, the investigator should then

    A. determine whether or not these witnesses were in communication with each other
    B. assume that such agreement means that the recollection was correct
    C. assume that the witnesses' observations were incorrect since two or more people usually will not agree on the same details
    D. question the witnesses again, concentrating on the details on which they differ

5.____

6. In trying to obtain a statement from a hospitalized individual who is unable to receive visitors, it would be BEST for an investigator

    A. draw up a statement from his own knowledge of the case and ask a hospital staff member to have the patient sign the statement when he is well
    B. contact the patient's family and arrange for an appointment to see the patient as soon as his condition permits
    C. leave a message at the hospital for the patient to contact him when he is available to receive visitors
    D. appear at the hospital with proper identification and request official permission from the hospital administrator to speak with the patient

6.____

7. Among employment specialists, it is generally agreed that the value of character references on employment applications is

    A. *limited,* chiefly because such references are written only by personal friends of the applicant
    B. *significant,* chiefly because information they transmit is unavailable from other sources
    C. *limited,* chiefly because they tend to give only favorable information
    D. *significant,* chiefly because they have direct knowledge of the applicant's abilities

7.____

8. The MOST important requirement of a person who is testifying about a criminal act that he witnessed is that he

    A. was conscious and attentive during the crime
    B. is a respected and trustworthy member of the community
    C. is without a prior criminal record
    D. gives a consistent account of the details of the crime

8.____

9. Assume that, after taking a written statement from Employee A, an investigator is about to obtain his signature. He wants to ask Employee B, a co-worker, to witness the signing but Employee B is not available at that time.
To expedite the investigation, it would be MOST desirable for the investigator to

    A. have Employee A sign the statement and obtain Employee B's signature at a later time
    B. ask an available disinterested party to witness Employee A's signature
    C. witness Employee A's signature himself
    D. have Employee A sign when Employee B is available

9.____

10. Witnesses are usually MOST willing to discuss an event when they are   10.____

    A. disinterested in the subsequent investigation
    B. interviewed immediately following the event
    C. interviewed for the first time
    D. known by the investigator

11. To determine the former addresses of a person who has moved several times within the   11.____
    same locality, it would be BEST to contact

    A. the Post Office   B. insurance companies
    C. public utilities   D. banking institutions

12. The one of the following that is CHARACTERISTIC of the interview as compared with the   12.____
    observation approach to investigation is that an interview generally

    A. requires more time to complete adequately
    B. is more likely to result in incomplete information
    C. is less applicable to the study of an individual's beliefs and values
    D. is less costly to conduct

13. The use of slang on the part of an investigator when questioning subjects is generally   13.____

    A. *inadvisable*; chiefly because it leads to misinterpretations
    B. *advisable*; chiefly because it will insure objective responses
    C. *inadvisable*; chiefly because it can compromise the investigator's dignity
    D. *advisable*; chiefly because it can promote ease of speech and understanding

14. Assume that a job applicant claims on his employment application that he has just   14.____
    recently become a United States citizen.
    Of the following, it would be MOST appropriate for you, in verifying this matter, to con-
    sult the

    A. Department of State   B. Treasury Department
    C. Immigration and Naturalization Service   D. Department of Justice

15. If an investigator receives an anonymous phone call from a person claiming to have   15.____
    knowledge of criminal behavior in an agency which is currently being investigated, the
    investigator should

    A. listen politely and make notes on the important facts given by the informant
    B. tell the informant what has already been discovered and ask if he has anything to
       add
    C. question the informant to obtain all the information he has
    D. ask the informant to submit his information in writing

16. When interviewing a child, an investigator should keep in mind the fact that children   16.____

    A. are psychologically incapable of giving an accurate statement
    B. usually have faulty perception
    C. are easily led into making incorrect statements since they tend to agree with the
       questioner
    D. will often make statements which are pure fantasy because they are not as obser-
       vant as adults

17. Following are three statements concerning the use of an investigator's notebook in court: 17.____

    I. A looseleaf-type notebook creates a more favorable impression in the court-room than a bound notebook because the former permits the removal of pages unrelated to the case in question

    II. An investigator's notebook should be written in ink, not pencil, because of the need for permanence

    III. The notebook should ideally contain the notes of only one investigation so that its scrutiny will not involve the disclosure of information relating to other investigations

Which of the following CORRECTLY classifies the above statements into those which are valid and those which are not valid?

    A. I and III are valid, but II is not.
    B. I and II are valid, but III is not.
    C. I is valid, but II and III are not.
    D. II and III are valid, but I is not.

18. The first three digits of a social security number are coded for the   18.____

    A. age of the cardholder when the card was issued
    B. cardholder's initials
    C. year the card was issued
    D. area in which the card was issued

19. Two methods of obtaining personal background information are the personal interview and the telephone inquiry.   19.____
As compared with the latter, the personal type of interview USUALLY _____ flexibility in questioning _____ frankness.

    A. permits; but discourages
    B. restricts; but encourages
    C. permits; and encourages
    D. restricts; and discourages

20. One of the important functions of investigators is to perform surveillances without the knowledge of the subject. If a subject thinks he is being followed, he is LEAST likely to react by   20.____

    A. reversing his course to see whether anyone else does likewise
    B. boarding a subway car and getting off just before it pulls out
    C. attempting to pass the surveillant several times to view him face-to-face
    D. using the services of a *convoy* to observe whether he is being followed

21. Assume that you are conducting an interview with a prospective employee who is of limited mental ability and low socio-economic status.   21.____
Of the following, it is MOST likely that asking him many open-ended questions about his work experience would cause him to respond

    A. articulately   B. reluctantly
    C. comfortably   D. aggressively

22. Assume, as an investigator, you want a witness to sign a statement.   22.____
Which of the following phrases is MOST likely to secure his signature?

    A. I would appreciate it if you would sign the statement at this time.
    B. Sign the statement where indicated.
    C. Sign the statement when you get the chance.
    D. If the statement is generally correct, please sign it.

23. During an interview, a subject makes statements an investigator knows to be false.   23.____
Of the following, it would be MOST appropriate for the investigator to

    A. point out each inconsistency in the subject's story as soon as the investigator detects it
    B. interrupt the subject and request that he submit to a polygraph test
    C. allow the subject to continue talking until he becomes enmeshed in his lies and then confront him with his falsehoods
    D. allow the subject to finish what he has to say and then explicitly inform him that it is a crime to lie to a government employee

24. One of the major objectives of a pre-employment interview is to get the interviewee to   24.____
respond freely to inquiries. The one of the following actions that would be MOST likely to
restrict the conversation of the interviewee would be for the investigator to

    A. keep a stenographic record of the interviewee's statements
    B. ask questions requiring complete explanations
    C. pose direct, specific questions to the interviewee
    D. allow the interviewee to respond to questions at his own pace

25. A list of the names, addresses, and titles of city employees is made available to the pub-   25.____
lic by the

    A. civil service commission
    B. comptroller's office
    C. mayor's office
    D. municipal reference and research center

―――――――

KEY (CORRECT ANSWERS)

1.	D	11.	C
2.	A	12.	D
3.	A	13.	D
4.	B	14.	C
5.	A	15.	C
6.	B	16.	C
7.	C	17.	D
8.	A	18.	D
9.	B	19.	C
10.	B	20.	C

21. B
22. B
23. C
24. A
25. D

EXAMINATION SECTION
TEST 1

DIRECTIONS: Each question or incomplete statement is followed by several suggested answers or completions. Select the one that BEST answers the question or completes the statement. *PRINT THE LETTER OF THE CORRECT ANSWER IN THE SPACE AT THE RIGHT.*

1. Assume you are supervising a group of investigators. Your unit is assigned a rush job requiring a special skill and overtime work.
Of the following, the MOST appropriate method of choosing the investigator to do this job is to

    A. assign the investigator who has the special skill required for the job
    B. ask an investigator who has previously indicated a willingness to work overtime
    C. call for a volunteer to perform this work
    D. offer the job to the investigator who is next in line to work overtime

1.____

2. Formal training programs can help remedy specific problems in an investigative unit. The one of the following that is NOT an intended result of such training programs is to

    A. eliminate the need for on-the-job training for new investigators
    B. help reduce the amount of overtime paid
    C. minimize the number of grievances made by investigators
    D. develop a pool of trained investigators needed for agency expansion

2.____

3. Periodic evaluation of subordinates' performance on the job serves all of the following purposes EXCEPT to

    A. point out weaknesses in performance to subordinates so that attempts can be made to eliminate them
    B. identify capable subordinates and insure that they are promoted
    C. indicate those subordinates who deserve training for greater responsibilities
    D. identify those subordinates who have exceptional ability

3.____

4. All of the following are proper objectives in the investigation of outside complaints about agency personnel EXCEPT the protection of the

    A. integrity and reputation of the staff
    B. public interest in identifying wrongdoers
    C. organization from liability resulting from unjust claims
    D. accused employees from disciplinary action

4.____

5. Assume that one of your subordinates had had a minor accident while performing a surveillance. In spite of your repeated demands, the subordinate refuses to prepare an accident report because he was only slightly injured. Of the following actions, it would be BEST in this situation for you to

    A. contact your superior to discuss disciplinary action
    B. have the employee file an affidavit absolving you of any responsibility for his injury
    C. ask the employee to submit a doctor's note to you on the extent of his injury
    D. call a meeting of subordinate personnel to discuss this situation

5.____

6. The one of the following that is likely to provide subordinates with the GREATEST satis-   6._____
faction on the job is

    A. compensation for overtime production
    B. challenging and interesting work
    C. compensation proportional to the amount of work produced
    D. minimum responsibility for the completion of work

7. An employee is GENERALLY considered guilty of insubordination when he   7._____

    A. refuses to obey a supervisor's order with which he disagrees
    B. declines to carry out a directive he genuinely believes will cause him personal injury
    C. uses foul or abusive language among other work group members
    D. reports to work late after being warned not do do so

8. The one of the following that is GENERALLY characteristic of the more effective supervi-   8._____
sors is that they

    A. specify every detail of the work to be done
    B. give subordinates leeway in the methods they use to complete their work
    C. supervise more closely than the less effective supervisors
    D. tend to be production-centered rather than employee-centered

9. If workers participate in planning, making important decisions, and the like, the supervi-   9._____
sor will lose prestige and his authority will deteriorate.
This statement is

    A. *true* because people have little respect for a leader who seeks their advice
    B. *true* because a supervisor must establish a firm command over his subordinates to be effective
    C. *false* because a skillful supervisor works with his subordinates to establish a goal and then works to reach it
    D. *false* because a supervisor gains prestige only by making all important decisions himself

10. As a supervisor, you note that while one of your subordinates does what he is told to do,   10._____
he seems disinterested and lacks motivation in performing his work.
Of the following, the BEST action for you to take to motivate this employee would be to

    A. transfer him to a more active unit
    B. give him less desirable work
    C. give him more responsibility
    D. assign him to work with a more experienced employee

11. Newly appointed supervisors will often assume responsibility for work which could be   11._____
handled by their subordinates.
Of the following, the MOST likely result of such a practice would be that the

    A. supervisor will gain the confidence of his subordinates
    B. subordinates' sense of initiative and responsibility will diminish
    C. supervisor will note an increase in the job satisfaction of his subordinates
    D. subordinates will have more time to learn more complex job skills

12. In order to accomplish the work of his unit MOST effectively, a supervisor of investigators   12._____
should

    A. do the important work himself
    B. assign complete responsibility for the completion of work only to his more produc-
        tive subordinates
    C. judiciously delegate authority to make decisions to his subordinates
    D. give sensitive and responsible work only to his most competent investigators

13. Assume, as a supervisor, you are approached by one of the investigators in your unit   13._____
with what you consider to be a minor grievance.
Of the following, the BEST way to handle this situation is to

    A. postpone taking any action since the passage of time usually resolves minor griev-
        ances
    B. try to resolve the problem immediately before it gets out of hand
    C. tell the investigator not to be concerned with minor grievances
    D. thank the investigator for calling the grievance to your attention and await further
        developments

14. Following are three guidelines a supervisor might follow in handling criticism by a supe-   14._____
rior:
       I. Consider the source of criticism before taking any action.
      II. Try to react calmly to criticism that is not justified.
     III. Analyze carefully only the criticism that requires a response.
Which of the following CORRECTLY classifies the above guidelines into those which
are valid and those which are not valid?

    A. I is valid, but II and III are not.
    B. I and II are valid, but III is not.
    C. II and III are valid, but I is not.
    D. III is valid, but I and III are not.

15. Assume that a supervisor notices that several of his subordinates, who are normally   15._____
punctual, have been late for work quite often during the last few months.
Which one of the following actions should the supervisor take FIRST in dealing with
this problem?

    A. Refer the matter to the personnel staff of his agency.
    B. Schedule counseling sessions on the need for being prompt.
    C. Review his own supervision to determine whether it has been adequate.
    D. Inform the subordinates that exact records of their latenesses are being kept.

16. Following are three statements concerning principles of delegation: 16._____
       I. Supervisors should not be held accountable for work that has been dele-
          gated to their subordinates.
      II. Subordinates should normally have only one line supervisor.
     III. When subordinates are given authority that is limited by factors such as
          departmental rules, their responsibility is also limited.
Which of the following BEST classifies the above statements into those that are valid
and those that are not valid?

A. I is valid, but II and III are not.
B. II is valid, but I and III are not.
C. I and II are valid, but III is not.
D. II and III are valid, but I is not.

17. Following are six steps that should be taken in the course of report preparation: 17.____
    I. Outlining the material for presentation in the report.
    II. Analyzing and interpreting the facts
    III. Analyzing the problem
    IV. Reaching conclusions
    V. Writing, revising, and rewriting the final copy
    VI. Collecting data
According to the principles of good report writing, the CORRECT order in which these steps should be taken is

A. VI, III, II, I, IV, V   B. III, VI, II, IV, I, V
C. III, VI, II, I, IV, V   D. VI, II, III, IV, I, V

18. Following are three statements concerning written reports: 18.____
    I. Clarity is generally more essential in oral reports than in written reports.
    II. Short sentences composed of simple words are generally preferred to complex sentences and difficult words.
    III. Abbreviations may be used whenever they are customary and will not distract the attention of the reader.
Which of the following choices CORRECTLY classifies the above statements into those which are valid and those which are not valid?

A. I and II are valid, but III is not valid.
B. I is valid, but II and III are not valid.
C. II and III are valid, but I is not valid.
D. III is valid, but I and II are not valid.

19. In order to produce a report written in a style that is both understandable and effective, an investigator should apply the principles of unity, coherence, and emphasis. The one of the following which is the BEST example of the principle of coherence is   19.____

A. interlinking sentences so that thoughts flow smoothly
B. having each sentence express a single idea to facilitate comprehension
C. arranging important points in prominent positions so they are not overlooked
D. developing the main idea fully to insure complete consideration

20. Following are three statements concerning public relations in a city agency: 20.____
    I. Public relations in an agency should be the sole responsibility of a trained public relations professional
    II. Public relations involves every contact the agency has with the public, whether the contact is in person or by letter or telephone
    III. The public should be told by the agency what it is going to do and how it is going to do it before hearing a version from other sources which may be distorted
Which of the following choices CORRECTLY classifies the above statements into those which are correct and those which are not?

A. I and II are correct, but III is not.
B. I is correct, but II and III are not.
C. II is correct, but I and III are not.
D. II and III are correct, but I is not.

21. Communication, both written and oral, is essential to the functioning of any organization.   21.____
    Written communication is generally more appropriate than oral communication when
    the information being transmitted

    A. concerns a small group of people
    B. has long-term significance
    C. is only of minimal importance
    D. is concise and simple to comprehend

22. Subordinates are MOST likely to accept changes in their work plans and schedules   22.____
    when their supervisor

    A. advises them that such changes must be implemented because they have been
        ordered by management
    B. gives them some background to help them understand the need for the changes
    C. tells them that even though he disagrees with the changes, they must be adhered
        to
    D. informs them he will follow up to determine how effective such changes are

Questions 23-25.

DIRECTIONS: Below is a report consisting of 15 numbered sentences, some of which are not
                consistent with the principles of good report writing. Questions 23 through 25
                are to be answered SOLELY on the basis of the information contained in the
                report and your knowledge of investigative principles and practices.

    To: Tom Smith, Administrative Investigator
    From: John Jones, Senior Investigator
    1. On January 7, I received a call from Mrs. H. Harris of 684 Sunset Street, Brooklyn.
    2. Mrs. Harris informed me that she wanted to report an instance of fraud relating to
        public assistance payments being received by her neighbor, Mrs. I. Wallace.
    3. I advised her that such a subject would best be discussed in person.
    4. I then arranged a field visitation for January 10 at Mrs. Harris' apartment, 684 Sun-
        set Street, Brooklyn.
    5. On January 10, I discussed the basis for Mrs. Harris' charge against Mrs. Wallace
        at the former's apartment.
    6. She stated that her neighbor is receiving Aid to Dependent Children payments for
        seven children, but that only three of her children are still living with her.
    7. In addition, Mrs. Harris also claimed that her husband, whom she reported to the
        authorities as missing, usually sees her several times a week.
    8. After further questioning, Mrs. Harris admitted to me that she had been quite
        friendly with Mrs. Wallace until they recently argued about trash left in their adjoin-
        ing hall corridor.
    9. However, she firmly stated that her allegations against Mr. Wallace were valid and
        that she feared repercussions for her actions.

10. At the completion of the interview, I assured Mrs. Harris of the confidentiality of her statements and that an attempt would be made to verify her allegations.
11. However, upon presentation of official identification, Mrs. Wallace refused to admit me to her apartment or grant an interview.
12. As I was leaving Mrs. Harris' apartment, I noticed a man, aged approximately 45, walking out of Mrs. Wallace's apartment.
13. I followed him until he entered a late model green Oldsmobile Cutlass, license plate #238DAB, and sped away.
14. On January 15, I returned to 684 Sunset Street, having determined that Mrs. Wallace is receiving assistance as indicated by Mrs. Harris.
15. I am, therefore, referring this matter to you for further instructions.

John Jones
Senior Investigator

23. The one of the following that indicates the MOST logical order for statements 11 through 15 is

23.____

A. 11, 12, 13, 14, 15
C. 11, 13, 14, 12, 15

B. 13, 14, 11, 12, 15
D. 12, 13, 14, 11, 15

24. Which of the following sentences from the report is ambiguous?
Sentence

24.____

A. 2
B. 7
C. 8
D. 9

25. Of the following, based on the above report and your knowledge of investigative practice, it is MOST likely that investigator Jones failed to obtain the desired information from Mrs. Wallace because

25.____

A. she was aware of Mrs. Harris' allegations
B. she was fearful of personal injury
C. he was not operating under cover
D. he had not made a prior arrangement for the visit

KEY (CORRECT ANSWERS)

1.	A	11.	B
2.	A	12.	C
3.	B	13.	B
4.	D	14.	B
5.	A	15.	C
6.	B	16.	B
7.	A	17.	B
8.	B	18.	C
9.	C	19.	A
10.	C	20.	D

21.	B
22.	B
23.	D
24.	B
25.	C

EXAMINATION SECTION
TEST 1

DIRECTIONS: Each question or incomplete statement is followed by several suggested answers or completions. Select the one that BEST answers the question or completes the statement. *PRINT THE LETTER OF THE CORRECT ANSWER IN THE SPACE AT THE RIGHT.*

1. The reliability of information obtained increases with the number of persons interviewed. The more the interviewees differ in their statements, the more persons it is necessary to interview to ascertain the true facts.
    According to this statement, the dependability of the information about an occurrence obtained from interviews is related to

    A.   how many people are interviewed
    B.   how soon after the occurrence an interview can be arranged
    C.   the individual technique of the interviewer
    D.   the interviewer's ability to detect differences in the statements of interviewees

1.____

2. A sufficient quantity of the material supplied as evidence enables the laboratory expert to determine the true nature of the substance, whereas an extremely limited specimen may be an abnormal sample containing foreign matter not indicative of the true nature of the material.
    On the basis of this statement alone, it may be concluded that a reason for giving an adequate sample of material for evidence to a laboratory expert is that

    A.   a limited specimen spoils more quickly than a larger sample
    B.   a small sample may not truly represent the evidence
    C.   he cannot analyze a small sample correctly
    D.   he must have enough material to keep a part of it untouched to show in court

2.____

Questions 3-4.

DIRECTIONS: Your answers to Questions 3 and 4 are to be based ONLY on the information given in the following paragraph.

Credibility of a witness is usually governed by his character and is evidenced by his reputation for truthfulness. Personal or financial reasons or a criminal record may cause a witness to give false information to avoid being implicated. Age, sex, physical and mental abnormalities, loyalty, revenge, social and economic status, indulgence in alcohol, and the influence of other persons are some of the many factors which may affect the accuracy, willingness, or ability with which witnesses observe, interpret, and describe occurrences.

3. According to the above paragraph, a witness may, for personal reasons, give wrong information about an occurrence because he

    A.   wants to protect his reputation for truthfulness
    B.   wants to embarrass the investigator
    C.   doesn't want to become involved
    D.   doesn't really remember what happened

3.____

4. According to the above paragraph, factors which influence the witness of an occurrence may affect

    4.____

    A. not only what he tells about it but what he was able and wanted to see of it
    B. only what he describes and interprets later but not what he actually sees at the time of the event
    C. what he sees but not what he describes
    D. what he is willing to see but not what he is able to see

5. *There are few individuals or organizations on whom some records are not kept.* This sentence means MOST NEARLY that

    5.____

    A. a few organizations keep most of the records on individuals
    B. some of the records on a few individuals are destroyed and not kept
    C. there are few records kept on individuals
    D. there is some kind of record kept on almost every individual

Questions 6-10.

DIRECTIONS: Questions 6 to 10 are based SOLELY on the following paragraph.

Those statutes of limitations which are of interest to a claim examiner are the ones affecting third party actions brought against an insured covered by a liability policy of insurance. Such statutes of limitations are legislative enactments limiting the time within which such actions at law may be brought. Research shows that such periods differ from state to state and vary within the states with the type of action brought. The laws of the jurisdiction in which the action is brought govern and determine the period within which the action may be instituted, regardless of the place of the cause of action or the residence of the parties at the time of cause of action. The period of time set by a statute of limitations for a tort action starts from the moment the alleged tort is committed. The period usually extends continuously until its expiration, upon which legal action may no longer be brought. However, there is a suspension of the running of the period when a defendant has concealed himself in order to avoid service of legal process. The suspension continues until the defendant discontinues his concealment, and then the period starts running again. A defendant may, by his agreement or conduct, be legally barred from asserting the statute of limitations as a defense to an action. The insurance carrier for the defendant may, by the misrepresentation of the claims man, cause such a bar against use of the statute of limitations by the defendant. If the claim examiner of the insurance carrier has by his conduct or assertion lulled the plaintiff into a false sense of security by false representations, the defendant may be barred from setting up the statute of limitations as a defense.

6. Of the following, the MOST suitable title for the above paragraph is:

    6.____

    A. Fraudulent Use of the Statute of Limitations
    B. Parties at Interest in a Lawsuit
    C. The Claim Examiner and the Law
    D. The Statute of Limitations in Claims Work

7. The period of time during which a third party action may be brought against an insured   7.____
   covered by a liability policy depends on

   A. the laws of the jurisdiction in which the action is brought
   B. where the cause of action which is the subject of the suit took place
   C. where the claimant lived at the time of the cause of action
   D. where the insured lived at the time of the cause of action

8. Time limits in third party actions which are set by the statutes of limitations described   8.____
   above are

   A. determined by claimant's place of residence at start of action
   B. different in a state for different actions
   C. the same from state to state for the same type of action
   D. the same within a state regardless of type of action

9. According to the above paragraph, grounds which may be legally used to prevent a   9.____
   defendant from using the statute of limitations as a defense in the action described are

   A. defendant's agreement or concealment; a charge of liability for death and injury
   B. defendant's agreement or conduct; misrepresentation by the claims man
   C. fraudulent concealment by claim examiner; a charge of liability for death or injury;
      defendant's agreement
   D. misrepresentation by claim examiner of carrier; defendant's agreement; plaintiff's
      concealment

10. Suppose an alleged tort was committed on January 1, 2003 and that the period in which   10.____
    action may be taken is set at three years by the statute of limitations. Suppose further
    that the defendant, in order to avoid service of legal process, had concealed himself from
    July 1, 2005 through December 31, 2005.
    In this case, the defendant may not use the statute of limitations as a defense unless
    action is brought by the plaintiff after

    A. January 1, 2006   B. February 28, 2006
    C. June 30, 2006   D. August 1, 2006

Questions 11-15.

DIRECTIONS: Your answers to Questions 11 to 15 must be based SOLELY on the informa-
              tion given in the following paragraph.

*The nature of the interview varies with the aim or the use to which it is put. While these
uses vary widely, interviews are basically of three types: fact-finding, informing, and motivating. One of these purposes usually predominates in an interview, but not to the exclusion of
the other two. If the main purpose is fact-finding, for example, the interviewer must often motivate the interviewee to cooperate in revealing the facts. A major factor in the interview is the
interaction of the personalities of the interviewer and the interviewee. The interviewee may
not wish to reveal the facts sought; or even though willing enough to impart them, he may not
be able to do so because of a lack of clear understanding as to what is wanted or because of
lack, of ability to put into words the information he has to give. On the other hand, the interviewer may not be able to grasp and report accurately the facts which the one being interviewed is trying to convey. Also, the interviewer's prejudice may make him not want to get at
the real facts or make him unable to recognize the truth.*

11. According to the above paragraph, the purpose of an interview   11._____

    A. determines the nature of the interview
    B. is usually the same for the three basic types of interviews
    C. is predominantly motivation of the interviewee
    D. is usually to check on the accuracy of facts previously obtained

12. In discussing the use or purpose of an interview, the above paragraph points out that   12._____

    A. a good interview should have only one purpose
    B. an interview usually has several uses that are equally important
    C. fact-finding should be the main purpose of an interview
    D. the interview usually has one main purpose

13. According to the above paragraph, an obstacle to the successful interview sometimes   13._____
attributable to the interviewee is

    A. a lack of understanding of how to conduct an interview
    B. an inability to express himself
    C. prejudice toward the interviewer
    D. too great a desire to please

14. According to the above paragraph, one way in which the interviewer may help the inter-   14._____
viewee to reveal the facts sought is to

    A. make him willing to impart the facts by stating clearly the consequences of false
       information
    B. make sure he understands what information is wanted
    C. motivate him by telling him how important he is in the investigation
    D. tell him what words to use to convey the information wanted

15. According to the above paragraph, bias on the part of the interviewer could   15._____

    A. be due to inability to understand the facts being imparted
    B. lead him to report the facts accurately
    C. make the interviewee unwilling to impart the truth
    D. prevent him from determining the facts

Questions 16-20.

DIRECTIONS: Your answers to Questions 16 to 20 are to be based SOLELY on the information given in the following paragraph.

PROCEDURE TO OBTAIN REIMBURSEMENT FROM DEPARTMENT OF HEALTH FOR CARE OF PHYSICALLY HANDICAPPED CHILDREN

Application for reimbursement must be received by the Department of Health within 30 days of the date of hospital admission in order that the Department of Hospitals may be reimbursed from the date of admission. Upon determination that patient is physically handicapped, as defined under Chapter 780 of the State Laws, the ward clerk shall prepare seven copies of Department of Health Form A-1 or A-2 Application and Authorization and shall submit six copies to the institutional Collections Unit. The ward clerk shall also initiate two copies of Department of Health Form B-1 or B-2 Financial and Social Report and shall forward them to the institutional Collections Unit for completion of Page 1 and routing to the Social Service Division for completion of the Social Summary on Page 2. Social Service Division shall return Form B-1 or B-2 to the institutional Collections Unit which shall forward one copy of Form B-1 or B-2 and six copies of Form A-1 or A-2 to Central Office Division of Collections for transmission to Bureau of Handicapped Children, Department of Health.

16. According to the above paragraph, the Department of Health will pay for hospital care for   16.____

    A. children who are physically handicapped
    B. any children who are ward patients
    C. physically handicapped adults and children
    D. thirty days for eligible children

17. According to the procedure described in the above paragraph, the definition of what constitutes a physical handicap is made by the   17.____

    A. attending physician   B. laws of the state
    C. Social Service Division   D. ward clerk

18. According to the above paragraph, Form B-1 or B-2 is   18.____

    A. a three page form containing detachable pages
    B. an authorization form issued by the Department of Hospitals
    C. completed by the ward clerk after the Social Summary has been entered
    D. sent to the institutional Collections Unit by the Social Service Division

19. According to the above paragraph, after their return by the Social Service Division, the institutional Collections Unit keeps   19.____

    A. one copy of Form A-1 or A-2
    B. one copy of Form A-1 or A-2 and one copy of Form B-1 or B-2
    C. one copy of Form B-1 or B-2
    D. no copies of Forms A-1 or A-2 or B-1 or B-2

20. According to the above paragraph, forwarding the Application and Authorization to the Department of Health is the responsibility of the   20.____

    A. Bureau for Handicapped Children
    B. Central Office Division of Collections
    C. Institutional Collections Unit
    D. Social Service Division

21. An investigator interviews members of the public at his desk. The attitude of the public toward this department will probably be LEAST affected by this investigator's   21.____

    A. courtesy   B. efficiency   C. height   D. neatness

22. While you are conducting an interview, the telephone on your desk rings. Of the following, it would be BEST for you to   22.____

    A. ask the interviewer at the next desk to answer your telephone and take the message for you
    B. excuse yourself, pick up the telephone, and tell the person on the other end you are busy and will call him back later

C. ignore the ringing telephone and continue with the interview
D. use another telephone to inform the operator not to put calls through to you while you are conducting an interview

23. An interviewee is at your desk, which is quite near to the desks where other people work. He beckons you a little closer and starts to talk in a low voice as though he does not want anyone else to hear him. Under these circumstances, the BEST thing for you to do is to   23.____

A. ask him to speak a little louder so that he can be heard
B. cut the interview short and not get involved in his problems
C. explain that people at other desks are not eavesdroppers
D. listen carefully to what he says and give it consideration

24. In the course of your work, you have developed a good relationship with the clerk in charge of the information section of a certain government agency from which you must frequently obtain information. This agency's procedures require that a number of long complicated forms be prepared by you before the information can be released.
For you to ask the clerk in charge to release information to you without your presenting the forms would be   24.____

A. *unwise,* mainly because the information so obtained is no longer considered official
B. *wise,* mainly because a great deal of time will be saved by you and by the clerk
C. *unwise,* mainly because it may impair the good relations you have established
D. *wise,* mainly because more information can usually be obtained through friendly contacts

25. Sometimes public employees are offered gifts by members of the public in an effort to show appreciation for acts performed purely as a matter of duty. An investigator to whom such a gift was offered refused to accept it.
The action of the investigator was   25.____

A. *bad;* the gift should have been accepted to avoid being rude to the person making the offer
B. *bad;* salaries paid public employees are not high enough to justify such refusals
C. *good;* he should accept such a gift only when he has done a special favor for someone
D. *good;* the acceptance of such gifts may raise doubts as to the honesty of the employee

26. From the point of view of current correct English usage and grammar, the MOST accept-   26.____
able of the following sentences is:

A. Each claimant was allowed the full amount of their medical expenses.
B. Either of the three witnesses is available.
C. Every one of the witnesses was asked to tell his story.
D. Neither of the witnesses are right.

27. From the point of view of current correct English usage and grammar, the MOST accept-   27.____
able of the following sentences is:

A. Beside the statement to the police, the witness spoke to no one.
B. He made no statement other than to the police and I.
C. He made no statement to any one else, aside from the police.
D. The witness spoke to no one but me.

28. From the point of view of current correct English usage and grammar, the MOST accept- 28.____
able of the following sentences is:

    A. The claimant has no one to blame but himself.
    B. The boss sent us, he and I, to deliver the packages.
    C. The lights come from mine and not his car.
    D. There was room on the stairs for him and myself.

29. Of the following excerpts, selected from letters, the one which is considered by modern 29.____
letter writing experts to be the BEST is:

    A. Attached please find the application form to be filled out by you. Return the form to
        this office at the above address.
    B. Forward to this office your cheek accompanied by the application form enclosed
        with this letter.
    C. If you wish to apply, please complete and return the enclosed form with your check.
    D. In reply to your letter of December --, enclosed herewith please find the application
        form you requested.

30. Which of the following sentences would be MOST acceptable, from the point of view of 30.____
current correct English usage and grammar, in a letter answering a request for information about eligibility for clinic care?

    A. Admission to this clinic is limited to patients' inability to pay for medical care.
    B. Patients who can pay little or nothing for medical care are treated in this clinic.
    C. The patient's ability to pay for medical care is the determining factor in his admissi-
        bility to this clinic.
    D. This clinic is for the patient's that cannot afford to pay or that can pay a little for
        medical care.

31. A city employee who writes a letter requesting information from a businessman should 31.____
realize that, of the following, it is MOST important to

    A. end the letter with a polite closing
    B. make the letter short enough to fit on one page
    C. use a form, such as a questionnaire, to save the businessman's time
    D. use a courteous tone that will get the desired cooperation

Questions 32-35.

DIRECTIONS: Each of Questions 32 to 35 consists of a sentence which may be classified
                appropriately under one of the following four categories:
                A. incorrect because of faulty grammar or sentence structure
                B. incorrect because of faulty punctuation
                C. incorrect because of faulty capitalization
                D. correct

                Examine each sentence carefully. Then, in the corresponding space at the
                right, print the letter preceding the category which is the BEST of the four sug-
                gested above. Each incorrect sentence contains only one type of error. Con-
                sider a sentence correct if it contains none of the types of errors mentioned,
                although there may be other correct ways of expressing the same thought.

32. Despite the efforts of the Supervising mechanic, the elevator could not be started.   32.____

33. The U.S. Weather Bureau, weather record for the accident date was checked.   33.____

34. John Jones accidentally pushed the wrong button and then all the lights went out.   34.____

35. The investigator ought to of had the witness sign the statement.   35.____

Questions 36-55.

DIRECTIONS: Each of Questions 36 to 55 consists of a word in capital letters followed by four suggested meanings of the word. For each question, choose the word or phrase which means MOST NEARLY the same as the word in capital letters.

36.   ABUT   36.____
   A.   abandon   B.   assist   C.   border on   D.   renounce

37.   ABSCOND   37.____
   A.   draw in   B.   give up   C.   refrain from   D.   deal off

38.   BEQUEATH   38.____
   A.   deaden   B.   hand down   C.   make sad   D.   scold

39.   BOGUS   39.____
   A.   sad   B.   false   C.   shocking   D.   stolen

40.   CALAMITY   40.____
   A.   disaster   B.   female   C.   insanity   D.   patriot

41.   COMPULSORY   41.____
   A.   binding   B.   ordinary   C.   protected   D.   ruling

42.   CONSIGN   42.____
   A.   agree with   B.   benefit   C.   commit   D.   drive down

43.   DEBILITY   43.____
   A.   failure   B.   legality   C.   quality   D.   weakness

44.   DEFRAUD   44.____
   A.   cheat   B.   deny   C.   reveal   D.   tie

45.   DEPOSITION   45.____
   A.   absence   B.   publication   C.   removal   D.   testimony

46. DOMICILE   46._____

    A. anger   B. dwelling   C. tame   D. willing

47. HEARSAY   47._____

    A. selfish   B. serious   C. rumor   D. unlikely

48. HOMOGENEOUS   48._____

    A. human   B. racial   C. similar   D. unwise

49. ILLICIT   49._____

    A. understood   B. uneven   C. unkind   D. unlawful

50. LEDGER   50._____

    A. book of accounts   B. editor
    C. periodica   D. shelf

51. NARRATIVE   51._____

    A. gossip   B. natural   C. negative   D. story

52. PLAUSIBLE   52._____

    A. reasonable   B. respectful   C. responsible   D. rightful

53. RECIPIENT   53._____

    A. absentee   B. receiver   C. speaker   D. substitute

54. SUBSTANTIATE   54._____

    A. appear for   B. arrange   C. confirm   D. combine

55. SURMISE   55._____

    A. aim   B. break   C. guess   D. order

Questions 56-60.

DIRECTIONS: In Questions 56 to 60, one of the four words is misspelled. For each question, choose the word which is misspelled.

56.   A. absence   B. accummulate   56._____
    C. acknowledgment   D. audible

57.   A. benificiary   B. disbursement   57._____
    C. exorbitant   D. incidentally

58.   A. inoculate   B. liaison   C. acquire   D. noticable   58._____

59.   A. peddler   B. permissible   C. persuade   D. pertenant   59._____

60.   A. reconcilation   B. responsable   60._____
    C. sizable   D. substantial

61. Suppose a badly cracked sidewalk, 160 feet long and 14 feet wide, is to be torn up and replaced in four equal sections.
Each section will _____ square feet.

61.____

    A. 40   B. 220   C. 560   D. 680

62. A businessman pays R dollars a month in rent, has a weekly payroll of P dollars, and a utility bill of U dollars for each two months.
His annual expenses can be expressed by

62.____

    A. 12 (R+P+U)   B. 52 (R+P+U)
    C. 12 (R+52P+6U)   D. 12 (R+4P+2U)

63. An interviewer can interview P number of people in H number of hours, including the time needed to prepare a report on each interview.
The number of people he can interview in a work week of W hours is represented by

63.____

    A. HW/P   B. PW/H   C. PH/W   D. 35H/P

64. Claims investigated by a certain unit total $8,430,000 for the year.
If the cost of investigating these claims is 17.3 cents per $100, the yearly cost of investigating these claims is MOST NEARLY

64.____

    A. $1,450   B. $14,500   C. $145,000   D. $1,450,000

65. Suppose that a business you are investigating presents the following figures:

65.____

year	Net income	Tax Rate on Net income
2001	$5,500	2%
2002	5,500	3%
2003	6,500	2%
2004	5,200	2 1/2%
2005	6,200	3%
2006	6,800	2 1/2%

According to these figures, it is MOST accurate to say that
    A. less tax was due in 2005 than in 2006
    B. more tax was due in 2001 than in 2004
    C. the same amount of tax was due in 2001 and 2002
    D. the same amount of tax was due in 2003 and 2004

66. In 1999, the number of investigations completed in a certain unit had increased 230 over the number completed in 1998, an increase of 10%. In 2000, the number completed decreased 10% from the number completed in 1999.
Therefore, the number of investigations completed in 2000 was _____ the number completed in 1998.

66.____

    A. 23 less than   B. 123 less than
    C. 230 more than   D. the same as

67. Assume that during a certain period, Unit A investigated 400 cases and Unit B investigated 300 cases.
If each unit doubled its number of investigations, the proportion of Unit A's investigations to Unit B's investigations would then be _____ it was.

67.____

    A. twice what   B. one-half as large as
    C. one-third larger than   D. the same as

68. In a certain family, the teenage daughter's annual earnings are 5/8 the earnings of her brother and 1/5 the earnings of her father.
If her brother earns $19,200 a year, then her father's annual earnings are

68.____

   A. $60,000   B. $75,000   C. $80,000   D. $96,000

69. Assume that, of the 1,700 verifications made by a certain investigating unit in a one-week period, 40% were birth records, 30% were military records, 10% were citizenship records, and the remainder were miscellaneous records. Then, the MOST accurate of the following statements about the relative number of different records is that

69.____

   A. citizenship records verifications equalled 20% of military record verifications
   B. fewer than 700 verifications were birth records
   C. miscellaneous records verifications were 20% more than citizenship records verifications
   D. more than 550 verifications were military records

70. Two units, A and B, answer, respectively, 1,000 and 1,500 inquiries a month. Assuming that the number of inquiries answered by Unit A increase at the rate of 20 each month, while those answered by Unit B decrease at the rate of 5 each month, the two units will answer the same number of inquiries at the end of _____ months.

70.____

   A. 10   B. 15   C. 20   D. 25

71. The interview is only one of the many investigatorial techniques used by the investigator for gathering information and evidence. Each such technique has its special use. The investigator *usually* finds the interview MOST suitable for getting

71.____

   A. facts or leads which are available only through individuals
   B. information available in documents and public records
   C. physical evidence relating to the subject of investigation
   D. information that people hesitate to put into writing

72. An investigator should consult his supervisor on a complicated problem before going ahead with his investigation. For an investigator to follow this advice would be

72.____

   A. *bad,* mainly because consultation is an admission of the investigator's weakness
   B. *good,* mainly because consultation is likely to lead to additional ideas on how to solve the problem
   C. *bad,* mainly because supervisors don't have time to discuss every problem with each investigator
   D. *good,* mainly because the responsibility for the investigation is shared with the supervisor

73. The general demeanor of the person being interviewed, what he says, and the way in which he says it, will usually give the investigator reliable clues concerning his character. It may be concluded from this statement that

73.____

   A. investigators usually become well-versed in applied psychology
   B. the behavior of the interviewee may give some indication of his character
   C. the investigator should be particularly on guard against deceit
   D. reliable people always show such reliability in their demeanor

74. Under the city charter, it is incumbent upon the Commissioner of Hospitals to collect for   74.____
the care and maintenance of a patient in an institution under the jurisdiction of the
Department if such patient is able to pay in whole or in part for such care and maintenance.
According to the preceding statement, it is MOST reasonable to assume that

    A. city hospitals are largely self-sufficient, medical services being donated and oper-
ating expenses being derived from income from patients
    B. city hospital facilities are intended for use only by the medically needy
    C. the duty of the Department of Hospitals to charge patients who are able to pay has
a legal basis
    D. the majority of patients in city institutions will not willingly pay for their care and
consistent efforts must be made to collect

75. In an experiment, a large group of people witnessed a certain incident. Half of the group   75.____
was then asked to write a detailed narrative report of what they had seen, while the other
half was given a lengthy questionnaire report on the incident to fill out. It was found that
the narrative reports covered a greater range of items and contained fewer errors of fact
than the question-answer reports.
It is MOST logical to conclude that in this experiment,

    A. narrative reports tended to be more accurate than question-answer reports
    B. question-answer reports tended to provide more details, while the narrative reports
contained more misstatements of fact
    C. some uncontrolled factor was at work since questionnaires usually elicit much
more information than this
    D. the range of questions in the questionnaire was narrow

76. During the course of an interview, it would be LEAST desirable for the investigator to   76.____

    A. correct immediately any grammatical errors made by an interviewee
    B. express himself in such a way as to be clearly understood
    C. restrict the interviewee to the subject of the interview
    D. make notes in a way that will not disturb the interviewee

77. Municipal hospitals which provide no services for private and semi-private patients shall   77.____
admit only medically needy persons unless refusal to admit a patient will constitute a
hazard to the public health or result in possible danger to the patient's life.
According to this statement, it is MOST logical to assume that

    A. medically needy persons may receive full medical services only in municipal hospi-
tals
    B. no municipal hospitals provide services for private and semi-private patients
    C. services for private and semi-private patients are provided by some municipal hos-
pitals
    D. voluntary and private hospitals provide services only for private and semi-private
patients

78. An investigator is making a neighborhood investigation to find additional witnesses to an   78.____
automobile accident that happened the day before at a corner in a district of buildings
with stores and offices above the stores. He started at 12 noon and stopped at a lunch
counter and every store in the vicinity of the accident that was open at the time of the
accident.
The investigator's procedure is

    A. *good;* he is likely to find people who were near the scene when the accident hap-
pened
    B. *good;* he will find the facts needed in the investigation
    C. *bad;* the investigator should have called first at the offices above the stores, as the
view was better from there
    D. *bad;* it is unlikely that people occupied with their business would notice an auto
accident outside

79. An investigator is interviewing a witness who has a speech difficulty. The witness is   79.____
becoming embarrassed because he has made several errors in telling his story.
Under these circumstances, it would be BEST for the investigator to

    A. call these errors rather sharply to the witness' attention so that he will use greater
care in describing the accident
    B. close the interview abruptly in order not to embarrass the witness further
    C. go through the motions of an interview for a while and then close it because this is
an unreliable witness
    D. try to ease his embarrassment and help him express himself

80. Some investigators prefer to type a statement to be signed by a witness. Others prefer to   80.____
write it out in longhand. One advantage of the handwritten statement as compared with a
typewritten statement is that a handwritten statement usually

    A. can be taken immediately while a typed statement cannot
    B. appears to be composed by the witness and so is more reliable
    C. eliminates any future question in court as to who prepared the statement
    D. is not likely to contain as many errors as a statement typed under stress

81. Some testimony cannot be accepted as a fact because the witness could not have per-   81.____
ceived personally the events he offers as facts in his testimony.
On this basis, which of the following statements by a witness is MOST acceptable as
fact?

    A. "Mr. Brown couldn't hear the horn."
    B. "He intended to call his wife."
    C. "There was no one at his home when he phoned."
    D. "The sidewalk was broken in the spot where he fell."

82. Strategy refers to the general plan or arrangement of the interview; tactics, to what is   82.____
said or done in the presence of the person being interviewed.
According to this definition, the one of the following which would be an example of
interview strategy is

    A. deciding the type of questions to be asked at the interview
    B. maintaining a sincere and reasonable manner

C. stating the purpose of the interview clearly and simply
D. wording a question precisely so that there is no misunderstanding as to what is meant

83. The prognosis of the patient's condition is the
83.____

    A. description of the patient's present condition
    B. opinion of the major cause of the illness
    C. statement of the expected course of the illness
    D. summary of secondary conditions

84. If a person's employment record indicates that he has never kept a job for any length of time, it is MOST likely that this person is a(n)
84.____

    A. part-time worker
    B. trouble maker
    C. unskilled worker
    D. unstable worker

85. In order to help a witness who has had very little education fully understand a statement he is to sign, the investigator, in preparing the statement, should
85.____

    A. have a notary public witness the preparation and signing of the statement
    B. typewrite the statement since uneducated persons find it hard to read handwritten statements
    C. use legal type questions and answers that are to the point
    D. use the same kind of language that the witness usually speaks

86. Mr. Brown acted out what he had seen happen and describedl what he was doing by saying, *"Richards was here. The door opened and hit him here – like this."* The investigator, who was recording the interview on tape at his office, said,
"Let me get this straight, Mr. Brown. Richards was standing sideways, two feet from the door, when the door opened, hitting Richard's elbow. Have I got it straight?" The witness replied, *"Right."*
The statement of the investigator under these circumstances was
86.____

    A. *bad;* it put words into the mouth of the witness
    B. *bad;* it merely duplicated what the witness had already shown
    C. *good;* it clarified a point that could confuse a listener to the tape
    D. *good;* it showed who was doing the interviewing

87. A significant fact to be remembered by the investigator in the course of his work is that a signed statement by a witness becomes evidence which
87.____

    A. can be used later to discredit any major change in the witness's story
    B. cannot be contradicted by other evidence
    C. cannot be used to induce the cla'imant to agree to a fair settlement
    D. is acceptable in court only if the signer cannot testify in court

88. Which of the following would usually be the BEST question for an investigator to ask a witness to find out what time he got to work?
88.____

    A. Did you get to work about 9 o'clock that morning?
    B. I suppose you arrived at the office late that morning?
    C. When did you get to work that day?
    D. You arrived at work late that morning! Can you tell me what time, please?

89. An investigator is examining the application of a 30-year-old applicant for a position.   89.____
Which of the following in his employment history for the past three years would indicate
the LEAST need for further investigation of this man's reliability as an employee?

   A. Many changes of employment, each to a position in another state at an equivalent
salary
   B. Frequent changes of employment to positions requiring skills the man had never
exercised before
   C. Few changes of employment but each change followed by six or more months of
unemployment
   D. Few changes of employment, each to a higher salary, with no unemployment

90. Security requirements for employment in defense plants have greatly expanded the num-   90.____
ber of sources of information about individuals.
According to the above statement, it is MOST valid to assume that

   A. increased sources of information exist for former defense plant employees
   B. detailed information is available on former defense plant employees
   C. information on former defense plant employees is limited to security information
   D. not much information is available on individuals who never worked in defense
plants

KEY (CORRECT ANSWERS)

1.	A	21.	C	41.	A	61.	C	81.	D
2.	B	22.	B	42.	C	62.	C	82.	A
3.	C	23.	D	43.	D	63.	B	83.	C
4.	A	24.	C	44.	A	64.	B	84.	D
5.	D	25.	D	45.	D	65.	D	85.	D
6.	D	26.	C	46.	B	66.	A	86.	C
7.	A	27.	D	47.	C	67.	D	87.	A
8.	B	28.	A	48.	C	68.	A	88.	C
9.	B	29.	C	49.	D	69.	B	89.	D
10.	C	30.	B	50.	A	70.	C	90.	A
11.	A	31.	D	51.	D	71.	A		
12.	D	32.	C	52.	A	72.	B		
13.	B	33.	B	53.	B	73.	B		
14.	B	34.	D	54.	C	74.	C		
15.	D	35.	A	55.	C	75.	A		
16.	A	36.	C	56.	B	76.	A		
17.	B	37.	D	57.	A	77.	C		
18.	D	38.	B	58.	D	78.	A		
19.	C	39.	B	59.	D	79.	D		
20.	B	40.	A	60.	B	80.	C		

EXAMINATION SECTION
TEST 1

DIRECTIONS: Each question or incomplete statement is followed by several suggested
answers or completions. Select the one that BEST answers the question or
completes the statement. *PRINT THE LETTER OF THE CORRECT ANSWER
IN THE SPACE AT THE RIGHT.*

1. An investigator uses *Forms A, B,* and *C* in filling out his investigation reports. He uses   1.____
    Form B five times as often as *Form A,* and he uses *Form C* three times as often as *Form B.*
    If the total number of all forms used by the investigator in a month equals 735, how
    many times was *Form B* used?

    A.   150   B.   175   C.   205   D.   235

2. Of all the investigators in one agency, 25% work in a particular building. Of these, 12%   2.____
    have desks on the 14th floor.
    What percentage of the investigators work in this building but do NOT have desks
    on the 14th floor?

    A.   12%   B.   13%   C.   22%   D.   23%

3. An investigator is given two reports to read. *Report P* is 160 pages long and takes the   3.____
    investigator 3 hours and 20 minutes to read.
    If *Report S* is 254 pages long and the investigator reads it at the same rate as he reads
    Report P, how long will it take him to read *Report S?* _____ hours _____ min-
    utes.

    A.   4; 15   B.   4; 50   C.   5; 10   D.   5; 30

4. A team of 6 investigators was assigned to interview 234 people.   4.____
    If half the investigators conduct twice as many interviews as the other half, and the
    slow group interviews 12 persons a day, how many days would it take to complete
    this assignment? _____ days.

    A.   4 1/2   B.   5   C.   6   D.   6 1/2

5. The investigators in one agency conduct an average of 12 interviews an hour from 10   5.____
    A.M. to 12 noon and from 1 P.M. to 5 P.M. daily. The director of this agency knows from
    past experience that 20% of those called in to be interviewed are unable to keep the
    appointments that were scheduled.
    If the director wants his staff to be kept occupied with interviews for the entire time
    period that has been set aside for this function, how many appointments should be
    scheduled for each day?

    A.   86   B.   90   C.   96   D.   101

6. An investigator has a 430 page report to read. The first day, he is able to read 20 pages.   6.____
    The second day, he reads 10 pages more than the first day, and the third day, he reads
    15 pages more than the second day.
    If, on the following days, he continues to read at the same rate he was reading on the
    third day, he will complete the report on the _____ day.

    A.   7th   B.   8th   C.   10th   D.   11th

7. The 36 investigators in an agency are each required to submit 25 investigation reports a week. These reports are filled out on a certain form, and only one copy of the form is needed per report.
Allowing 20% for waste, how many packages of 45 forms a piece should be ordered for each weekly period?

    A. 15   B. 20   C. 25   D. 30

7.____

8. During the fiscal year, an investigative unit received $260 for stationery and telephone expenditures. It spent 43% for stationery and 1/3 of the balance for telephone service. The amount of money that was left at the end of the fiscal year was MOST NEARLY

    A. $49   B. $50   C. $99   D. $109

8.____

Questions 9-10.

DIRECTIONS: Answer Questions 9 and 10 SOLELY on the data given below.

Number of days absent per worker (sickness)	1	2	3	4	5	6	7	8 or Over
Number of workers	96	45	16	3	1	0	1	0

Total Number of Workers: 500
Period Covered: Jan. 1, 2015 - Dec. 31, 2015

9. The TOTAL number of man days lost due to illness in 2015 was

    A. 137   B. 154   C. 162   D. 258

9.____

10. Of the 500 workers studied, the number who lost NO days due to sickness in 2015 was

    A. 230   B. 298   C. 338   D. 372

10.____

Questions 11-13.

DIRECTIONS: Answer Questions 11 to 13 SOLELY on the basis of the following paragraphs.

The rise of urban-industrial society has complicated the social arrangements needed to regulate contacts between people. As a consequence, there has been an unprecedented increase in the volume of laws and regulations designed to control individual conduct and to govern the relationship of the individual to others. In a century, there has been an eight-fold increase in the crimes for which one may be prosecuted.

For these offenses, the courts have the ultimate responsibility for redressing wrongs and convicting the guilty. The body of legal precepts gives the impression of an abstract and evenhanded dispensation of justice. Actually, the personnel of the agencies applying these precepts are faced with the difficulties of fitting abstract principles to highly variable situations emerging from the dynamics of everyday life. It is inevitable that discrepancies should exist between precept and practice.

The legal institutions serve as a framework for the social order by their slowness to respond to the caprices of transitory fad. This valuable contribution exacts a price in terms of the inflexibility of legal institutions in responding to new circumstances. This possibility is pro-moted by the changes in values and norms of the dynamic larger culture of which the legal precepts are a part.

11. According to the above passage, the increase in the number of laws and regulations dur-ing the twentieth century can be attributed to the

    11.____

    A. complexity of modern industrial society
    B. increased seriousness of offenses committed
    C. growth of individualism
    D. anonymity of urban living

12. According to the above passage, which of the following presents a problem to the staff of legal agencies? The

    12.____

    A. need to eliminate the discrepancy between precept and practice
    B. necessity to apply abstract legal precepts to rapidly changing conditions
    C. responsibility for reducing the number of abstract legal principles
    D. responsibility for understanding offenses in terms of the real-life situations from which they emerge

13. According to the above passage, it can be concluded that legal institutions affect social institutions by

    13.____

    A. preventing change
    B. keeping pace with its norms and values
    C. changing its norms and values
    D. providing stability

Questions 14-16.

DIRECTIONS: Answer Questions 14 through 16 SOLELY on the basis of information given in the passage below.

A personnel interviewer, selecting job applicants, may find that he reacts badly to some people even on first contact. This reaction cannot usually be explained by things that the interviewee has done or said. Most of us have had the experience of liking or disliking, of feel-ing comfortable or uncomfortable with people on first acquaintance, long before we have had a chance to make a conscious, rational decision about them. Often, too, our liking or disliking is transmitted to the other person by subtle processes such as gestures, posture, voice intonations, or choice of words. The point to be kept in mind is this: the relations between people are complex and occur at several levels, from the conscious to the unconscious. This is true whether the relationship is brief or long, formal or informal.

Some of the major dynamics of personality which operate on the unconscious level are projection, sublimation, rationalization, and repression. Encountering these for the first time, one is apt to think of them as representing pathological states. In the extreme, they undoubt-edly are, but they exist so universally that we must consider them also to be parts of normal personality.

Without necessarily subscribing to any of the numerous theories of personality, it is possible to describe personality in terms of certain important aspects or elements. We are all aware of ourselves as thinking organisms.

This aspect of personality, the conscious part, is important for understanding human behavior, but it is not enough. Many find it hard to accept the notion that each person also has an unconscious. The existence of the unconscious is no longer a matter of debate. It is not possible to estimate at all precisely What proportion of our total psychological life is conscious, what proportion unconscious. Everyone who has studied the problem, however, agrees that consciousness is the smaller part of personality. Most of what we are and do is a result of unconscious processes. To ignore this is to risk mistakes.

14. The passage above suggests that an interviewer can be MOST effective if he   14._____

    A. learns how to determine other peoples' unconscious motivations
    B. learns how to repress his own unconsciously motivated mannerisms and behavior
    C. can keep others from feeling that he either likes or dislikes them
    D. gains an understanding of how the unconscious operates in himself and in others

15. It may be inferred from the passage above that the *subtle processes such as gestures,*   15._____
    posture, voice intonation, or choice of words referred to in the first paragraph are USU-
    ALLY

    A. in the complete control of an expert investigator
    B. the determining factors in the friendships a person establishes
    C. controlled by a person's unconscious
    D. not capable of being consciously controlled

16. The passage above implies that various different personality theories are USUALLY   16._____

    A. so numerous and different as to be valueless to an investigator
    B. in basic agreement about the importance of the unconscious
    C. understood by the investigator who strives to be effective
    D. in agreement that personality factors such as projection and repression are patho-
       logical

Questions 17-19.

DIRECTIONS: Questions 17 through 19 are to be answered SOLELY on the basis of informa-
               tion contained in the following passage.

No matter how well the interrogator adjusts himself to the witness and how precisely he induces the witness to describe his observations, mistakes still can be made. The mistakes made by an experienced interrogator may be comparatively few, but as far as the witness is concerned, his path is full of pitfalls. Modern "witness psychology" has shown that even the most honest and trustworthy witnesses are apt to make grave mistakes in good faith. It is, therefore, necessary that the interrogator, get an idea of the weak links in the testimony in order to check up on them in the event that something appears to be strange or not quite satisfactory.

Unfortunately, modern witness psychology does not yet offer any means of directly testing the credibility of testimony. It lacks precision and method, in spite of worthwhile attempts on the part of learned men. At the same time, witness psychology, through the gathering of many experiences concerning the weaknesses of human testimony, has been of invaluable service. It shows clearly that only evidence of a technical nature has absolute value as proof.

Testimony may be separated into the following stages: (1) perception; (2) observation; (3) mind fixation of the observed occurrences, in which fantasy, association of ideas, and personal judgment participate; (4) expression in oral or written form, where the testimony is transferred from one witness to another or to the interrogator.

Each of these stages offers innumerable possibilities for the distortion of testimony.

17. The passage above indicates that having witnesses talk to each other before testifying is a practice which is GENERALLY   17.____

    A. *desirable,* since the witnesses will be able to correct each other's errors in observation before testimony
    B. *undesirable,* since the witnesses will collaborate on one story to tell the investigator
    C. *undesirable,* since one witness may distort his testimony because of what another witness may erroneously say
    D. *desirable,* since witnesses will become aware of discrepancies in their own testimony and can point out the discrepancies to the investigator

18. According to the above passage, the one of the following which would be the MOST reliable for use as evidence would be the testimony of a   18.____

    A. handwriting expert about a signature on a forged check
    B. trained police officer about the identity of a criminal
    C. laboratory technician about an accident he has observed
    D. psychologist who has interviewed any witnesses who relate conflicting stories

19. Concerning the validity of evidence, it is clear from the above passage that   19.____

    A. only evidence of a technical nature is at all valuable
    B. the testimony of witnesses is so flawed that it is usually valueless
    C. an investigator, by knowing modern witness psychology, will usually be able to perceive mistaken testimony
    D. an investigator ought to expect mistakes in even the most reliable witness testimony

Questions 20-21.

DIRECTIONS: Answer Questions 20 and 21 SOLELY on the basis of information given in the passage below.

Since we generally assure informants that what they say is confidential, we are not free to tell one informant what the other has told us. Even if the informant says, "I don't care who knows it; tell anybody you want to," we find it wise to treat the interview as confidential. An interviewer who relates to some informants what other informants have told him is likely to stir up anxiety and suspicion. Of course, the interviewer may be able to tell an informant what he has heard without revealing the source of his information. This may be perfectly appropriate where a story has wide currency so that an informant cannot infer the source of the informa-

tion. But if an event is not widely known, the mere mention of it may reveal to one informant what another informant has said about the situation. How can the data be cross-checked in these circumstances?

20. The passage above IMPLIES that the anxiety and suspicion an interviewer may arouse by telling what has been learned in other interviews is due to the

    20.____

    A. lack of trust the person interviewed may have in the interviewer's honesty
    B. troublesome nature of the material which the interviewer has learned in other interviews
    C. fact that the person interviewed may not believe that permission was given to repeat the information
    D. fear of the person interviewed that what he is telling the interviewer will be repeated

21. The paragraph above is MOST likely part of a longer passage dealing with

    21.____

    A. ways to verify data gathered in interviews
    B. the various anxieties a person being interviewed may feel
    C. the notion that people sometimes say things they do not mean
    D. ways an interviewer can avoid seeming suspicious

Questions 22-23.

DIRECTIONS: Answer Questions 22 and 23 SOLELY on the basis of information given below.

The ability to interview rests not on any single trait, but on a vast complex of them. Habits, skills, techniques, and attitudes are all involved. Competence in interviewing is acquired only after careful and diligent study, prolonged practice (preferably under supervision), and a good bit of trial and error; for interviewing is not an exact science, it is an art. Like many other arts, however, it can and must draw on science in several of its aspects.

There is always a place for individual initiative, for imaginative innovations, and for new combinations of old approaches. The skilled interviewer cannot be bound by a set of rules. Likewise, there is not a set of rules which can guarantee to the novice that his interviewing will be successful. There are, however, some accepted, general guideposts which may help the beginner to avoid mistakes, learn how to conserve his efforts, and establish effective working relationships with interviewees; to accomplish, in short, what he sets out to do.

22. According to the passage above, rules and standard techniques for interviewing are

    22.____

    A. helpful for the beginner, but useless for the experienced, innovative interviewer
    B. destructive of the innovation and initiative needed for a good interviewer
    C. useful for even the experienced interviewer, who may, however, sometimes go beyond them
    D. the means by which nearly anybody can become an effective interviewer

23. According to the passage above, the one of the following which is a prerequisite to competent interviewing is

    23.____

    A. avoid mistakes   B. study and practice
    C. imaginative innovation   D. natural aptitude

Questions 24-27.

DIRECTIONS: Answer Questions 24 through 27 SOLELY on the basis of information given in
the following paragraph.

*The question of what material is relevant is not as simple as it might seem. Frequently,
material which seems irrelevant to the inexperienced has, because of the common tendency
to disguise and distort and misplace one's feelings, considerable significance. It may be necessary to let the client "ramble on" for a while in order to clear the decks, as it were, so that he
may get down to things that really are on his mind. On the other hand, with an already dis-
turbed person, it may be important for the interviewer to know when to discourage further
elaboration of upsetting material. This is especially the case where the worker would be
unable to do anything about it. An inexperienced interviewer might, for instance, be intrigued
with the bizarre elaboration of material that the psychotic produces, but further elaboration of
this might encourage the client in his instability. A too random discussion may indicate that
the interviewee is not certain in what areas the interviewer is prepared to help him, and he
may be seeking some direction. Or again, satisfying though it may be for the interviewer to
have the interviewee tell him intimate details, such revelations sometimes need to be
checked or encouraged only in small doses. An interviewee who has "talked too much" often
reveals subsequent anxiety. This is illustrated by the fact that frequently after a "confessional"
interview, the interviewee surprises the interviewer by being withdrawn, inarticulate, or hos-
tile, or by breaking the next appointment.*

24.   Sometimes a client may reveal certain personal information to an interviewer and subse-   24.____
quently may feel anxious about this revelation.
If, during an interview, a client begins to discuss very personal matters, it would be
BEST to

    A.   tell the client, in no uncertain terms, that you're not interested in personal details
    B.   ignore the client at this point
    C.   encourage the client to elaborate further on the details
    D.   inform the client that the information seems to be very personal

25.   The author indicates that clients with severe psychological disturbances pose an espe-   25.____
cially difficult problem for the inexperienced interviewer.
The difficulty lies in the possibility of the client

    A.   becoming physically violent and harming the interviewer
    B.   *rambling on* for a while
    C.   revealing irrelevant details which may be followed by cancelled appointments
    D.   reverting to an unstable state as a result of interview material

26.   An interviewer should be constantly alert to the possibility of obtaining clues from the cli-   26.____
ent as to the problem areas.
According to the above passage, a client who discusses topics at random may be

    A.   unsure of what problems the interviewer can provide help with
    B.   reluctant to discuss intimate details
    C.   trying to impress the interviewer with his knowledge
    D.   deciding what relevant material to elaborate on

27. The evaluation of a client's responses may reveal substantial information that may aid the   27._____
interviewer in assessing the problem areas that are of concern to the client. Responses
that seemed irrelevant at the time of the interview may be of significance because

     A.   considerable significance is attached to all irrelevant material
     B.   emotional feelings are frequently masked
     C.   an initial *rambling on* is often a prelude to what is actually bothering the client
     D.   disturbed clients often reveal subsequent anxiety

Questions 28-30.

DIRECTIONS: Answer Questions 28 through 30 SOLELY on the basis of the following paragraph.

*The physical setting of the interview may determine its entire potentiality. Some degree
of privacy and a comfortable relaxed atmosphere are important. The interviewee is not
encouraged to give much more than his name and address if the interviewer seems busy with
other things, if people are rushing about, if there are distracting noises. He has a right to feel
that, whether the interview lasts five minutes or an hour, he has, for that time, the undivided
attention of the interviewer. Interruptions, telephone calls, and so on, should be reduced to a
minimum. If the interviewee has waited in a crowded room for what seems to him an intermi-
nably long period, he is naturally in no mood to sit down and discuss what is on his mind.
Indeed, by that time, the primary thing on his mind may be his irritation at being kept waiting,
and he frequently feels it would be impolite to express this. If a wait or interruptions have
been unavoidable, it is always helpful to give the client some recognition that these are disturbing and that we can naturally understand that they make it more difficult for him to proceed. At the same time, if he protests that they have not troubled him, the interviewer can
best accept his statements at their face value, as further insistence that they must have been
disturbing may be interpreted by him as accusing, and he may conclude that the interviewer
has been personally hurt by his irritation.*

28. Distraction during an interview may tend to limit the client's responses.   28._____
In a case where an interruption has occurred, it would be BEST for the investigator to

     A.   terminate this interview and have it rescheduled for another time period
     B.   ignore the interruption since it is not continuous
     C.   express his understanding that the distraction can cause the client to feel disturbed
     D.   accept the client's protests that he has been troubled by the interruption

29. To maximize the rapport that can be established with the client, an appropriate physical   29._____
setting is necessary. At the very least, some privacy would be necessary.
In addition, the interviewer should

     A.   always appear to be busy in order to impress the client
     B.   focus his attention only on the client
     C.   accept all the client's statements as being valid
     D.   stress the importance of the interview to the client

30. Clients who have been waiting quite some time for their interview may, justifiably, become upset.
However, a client may initially attempt to mask these feelings because he may

    A. personally hurt the interviewer
    B. want to be civil
    C. feel that the wait was unavoidable
    D. fear the consequences of his statement

30.____

KEY (CORRECT ANSWERS)

1.	B	11.	A	21.	A
2.	C	12.	B	22.	C
3.	D	13.	D	23.	B
4.	D	14.	D	24.	D
5.	B	15.	C	25.	D
6.	D	16.	B	26.	A
7.	C	17.	C	27.	B
8.	C	18.	A	28.	C
9.	D	19.	D	29.	B
10.	C	20.	D	30.	B

TEST 2

Each question or incomplete statement is followed by several suggested answers or completions. Select the one that BEST answers the question or completes the statement. *PRINT THE LETTER OF THE CORRECT ANSWER IN THE SPACE AT THE RIGHT.*

Questions 1-5.

DIRECTIONS   In Questions 1 through 5, choose the sentence which is BEST from the point of view of English usage suitable for a business report.

1.   A.   The client's receiving of public assistance checks at two different addresses were   1.____
           disclosed by the investigation.
      B.   The investigation disclosed that the client was receiving public assistance
           checks at two different addresses.
      C.   The client was found out by the investigation to be receiving public assistance
           checks at two different addresses.
      D.   The client has been receiving public assistance checks at two different
           addresses, disclosed the investigation.

2.   A.   The investigation of complaints are usually handled by this unit, which deals with   2.____
           internal security problems in the department.
      B.   This unit deals with internal security problems in the department; usually investi-
           gating complaints.
      C.   Investigating complaints is this unit's job, being that it handles internal security
           problems in the department.
      D.   This unit deals with internal security problems in the department and usually
           investigates complaints.

3.   A.   The delay in completing this investigation was caused by difficulty in obtaining the   3.____
           required documents from the candidate.
      B.   Because of difficulty in obtaining the required documents from the candidate is
           the reason that there was a delay in completing this investigation.
      C.   Having had difficulty in obtaining the required documents from the candidate,
           there was a delay in completing this investigation.
      D.   Difficulty in obtaining the required documents from the candidate had the affect
           of delaying the completion of this investigation.

4.   A.   This report, together with documents supporting our recommendation, are being   4.____
           submitted for your approval.
      B.   Documents supporting our recommendation is being submitted with the report
           for your approval.
      C.   This report, together with documents supporting our recommendation, is being
           submitted for your approval.
      D.   The report and documents supporting our recommendation is being submitted
           for your approval.

5. A. Several people were interviewed and numerous letters were sent before this case   5.____
       was completed.
    B. Completing this case, interviewing several people and sending numerous letters
       were necessary.
    C. To complete this case needed interviewing several people and sending numer-
       ous letters.
    D. Interviewing several people and sending numerous letters was necessary to
       complete the case.

Questions 6-20.

DIRECTIONS: For each of the sentences numbered 6 to 20, select from the options given
              below the MOST applicable choice, and mark your answer accordingly.
    A. The sentence is correct.
    B. The sentence contains a spelling error only.
    C. The sentence contains an English grammar error only.
    D. The sentence contains both a spelling error and an English grammar
       error.

6. He is a very dependible person whom we expect will be an asset to this division.   6.____

7. An investigator often finds it necessary to be very diplomatic when conducting an inter-   7.____
    view.

8. Accurate detail is especially important if court action results from an investigation.   8.____

9. The report was signed by him and I since we conducted the investigation jointly.   9.____

10. Upon receipt of the complaint, an inquiry was begun.   10.____

11. An employee has to organize his time so that he can handle his workload efficiantly.   11.____

12. It was not apparant that anyone was living at the address given by the client.   12.____

13. According to regulations, there is to be at least three attempts made to locate the client.   13.____

14. Neither the inmate nor the correction officer was willing to sign a formal statement.   14.____

15. It is our opinion that one of the persons interviewed were lying.   15.____

16. We interviewed both clients and departmental personel in the course of this investiga-   16.____
    tion.

17. It is concievable that further research might produce additional evidence.   17.____

18. There are too many occurences of this nature to ignore.   18.____

19. We cannot accede to the candidate's request.   19.____

20. The submission of overdue reports is the reason that there was a delay in completion of   20.____
    this investigation.

Questions 21-25.

DIRECTIONS: Each of Questions 21 to 25 consists of three sentences lettered A, B, and C. In each of these questions, one of the sentences may contain an error in grammar, sentence structure, or punctuation, or all three sentences may be correct. If one of the sentences in a question contains an error in grammar, sentence structure, or punctuation, print in the space on the right the capital letter preceding the sentence which contains the error. If all three sentences are correct, print the letter D.

21. A. Mr. Smith appears to be less competent than I in performing these duties.   21.____
    B. The supervisor spoke to the employee, who had made the error, but did not reprimand him.
    C. When he found the book lying on the table, he immediately notified the owner.

22. A. Being locked in the desk, we were certain that the papers would not be taken.   22.____
    B. It wasn't I who dictated the telegram; I believe it was Eleanor.
    C. You should interview whoever comes to the office today.

23. A. The clerk was instructed to set the machine on the table before summoning the manager.   23.____
    B. He said that he was not familiar with those kind of activities.
    C. A box of pencils, in addition to erasers and blotters, was included in the shipment of supplies.

24. A. The supervisor remarked, "Assigning an employee to the proper type of work is not always easy."   24.____
    B. The employer found that each of the applicants were qualified to perform the duties of the position.
    C. Any competent student is permitted to take this course if he obtains the consent of the instructor.

25. A. The prize was awarded to the employee whom the judges believed to be most deserving.   25.____
    B. Since the instructor believes this book is the better of the two, he is recommending it for use in the school.
    C. It was obvious to the employees that the completion of the task by the scheduled date would require their working overtime.

KEY (CORRECT ANSWERS)

1.	B		11.	B
2.	D		12.	B
3.	A		13.	C
4.	C		14.	A
5.	A		15.	C
6.	D		16.	B
7.	A		17.	B
8.	A		18.	B
9.	C		19.	A
10.	A		20.	C

21.	B
22.	A
23.	B
24.	B
25.	D

PREPARING WRITTEN MATERIAL

EXAMINATION SECTION
TEST 1

Questions 1-15.

DIRECTIONS: For each of Questions 1 through 15, select from the options given below the MOST applicable choice, and mark your answer accordingly.

    A. The sentence is correct.
    B. The sentence contains a spelling error *only.*
    C. The sentence contains an English grammar error *only.*
    D. The sentence contains both a spelling error and an English grammar error.

1. He is a very dependible person whom we expect will be an asset to this division.   1._____

2. An investigator often finds it necessary to be very diplomatic when conducting an interview.   2._____

3. Accurate detail is especially important if court action results from an investigation.   3._____

4. The report was signed by him and I since we conducted the investigation jointly.   4._____

5. Upon receipt of the complaint, an inquiry was begun.   5._____

6. An employee has to organize his time so that he can handle his workload efficiantly.   6._____

7. It was not apparant that anyone was living at the address given by the client.   7._____

8. According to regulations, there is to be at least three attempts made to locate the client.   8._____

9. Neither the inmate nor the correction officer was willing to sign a formal statement.   9._____

10. It is our opinion that one of the persons interviewed were lying.   10._____

11. We interviewed both clients and departmental personel in the course of this investigation.   11._____

12. It is concievable that further research might produce additional evidence.   12._____

13. There are too many occurences of this nature to ignore.   13._____

14. We cannot accede to the candidate's request.   14._____

15. The submission of overdue reports is the reason that there was a delay in completion of this investigation.   15._____

Questions 16-25.

DIRECTIONS: Each of Questions 16 through 25 may be classified under one of the following four categories:

    A. Faulty because of incorrect grammar or sentence structure
    B. Faulty because of incorrect punctuation
    C. Faulty because of incorrect spelling
    D. Correct

Examine each sentence carefully to determine under which of the above four options it is best classified. Then, in the space at the right, write the letter preceding the option which is the BEST of the four suggested above. Each incorrect sentence contains but one type of error. Consider a sentence to be correct if it contains none of the types of errors mentioned, even though there may be other correct ways of expressing the same thought.

16. Although the department's supply of scratch pads and stationary have diminished considerably, the allotment for our division has not been reduced.   16._____

17. You have not told us whom you wish to designate as your secretary.   17._____

18. Upon reading the minutes of the last meeting, the new proposal was taken up for consideration.   18._____

19. Before beginning the discussion, we locked the door as a precautionery measure.   19._____

20. The supervisor remarked, "Only those clerks, who perform routine work, are permitted to take a rest period."   20._____

21. Not only will this duplicating machine make accurate copies, but it will also produce a quantity of work equal to fifteen transcribing typists.   21._____

22. "Mr. Jones," said the supervisor, "we regret our inability to grant you an extention of your leave of absence."   22._____

23. Although the employees find the work monotonous and fatigueing, they rarely complain.   23._____

24. We completed the tabulation of the receipts on time despite the fact that Miss Smith our fastest operator was absent for over a week.   24._____

25. The reaction of the employees who attended the meeting, as well as the reaction of those who did not attend, indicates clearly that the schedule is satisfactory to everyone concerned.   25._____

———

KEY (CORRECT ANSWERS)

1.	D		11.	B
2.	A		12.	B
3.	A		13.	B
4.	C		14.	A
5.	A		15.	C
6.	B		16.	A
7.	B		17.	D
8.	C		18.	A
9.	A		19.	C
10.	C		20.	B

21.	A
22.	C
23.	C
24.	B
25.	D

TEST 2

DIRECTIONS: Questions 1 through 15 consist of two sentences. Some are correct according to ordinary formal English usage. Others are incorrect because they contain errors in English usage, spelling, or punctuation. Consider a sentence correct if it contains no errors in English usage, spelling, or punctuation, even if there may be other ways of writing the sentence correctly. Mark your answer:

A. If only sentence I is correct
B. If only sentence II is correct
C. If sentences I and II are correct
D. If neither sentence I nor II is correct

1.   I. The influence of recruitment efficiency upon administrative standards is readily apparant.
     II. Rapid and accurate thinking are an essential quality of the police officer.

1.____

2.   I. The administrator of a police department is constantly confronted by the demands of subordinates for increased personnel in their respective units.
     II. Since a chief executive must work within well-defined fiscal limits, he must weigh the relative importance of various requests.

2.____

3.   I. The two men whom the police arrested for a parking violation were wanted for robbery in three states.
     II. Strong executive control from the top to the bottom of the enterprise is one of the basic principals of police administration.

3.____

4.   I. When he gave testimony unfavorable to the defendant loyalty seemed to mean very little.
     II. Having run off the road while passing a car, the patrolman gave the driver a traffic ticket.

4.____

5.   I. The judge ruled that the defendant's conversation with his doctor was a priviliged communication.
     II. The importance of our training program is widely recognized; however, fiscal difficulties limit the program's effectiveness.

5.____

6.   I. Despite an increase in patrol coverage, there were less arrests for crimes against property this year.
     II. The investigators could hardly have expected greater cooperation from the public.

6.____

7.   I. Neither the patrolman nor the witness could identify the defendant as the driver of the car.
     II. Each of the officers in the class received their certificates at the completion of the course.

7.____

8.   I. The new commander made it clear that those kind of procedures would no longer   8.____
be permitted.
     II. Giving some weight to performance records is more advisable then making pro-
motions solely on the basis of test scores.

9.   I. A deputy sheriff must ascertain whether the debtor, has any property.   9.____
     II. A good deputy sheriff does not cause histerical excitement when he executes a
process.

10.   I. Having learned that he has been assigned a judgment debtor, the deputy sheriff   10.____
should call upon him.
     II. The deputy sheriff may seize and remove property without requiring a bond.

11.   I. If legal procedures are not observed, the resulting contract is not enforseable.   11.____
     II. If the directions from the creditor's attorney are not in writing, the deputy sheriff
should request a letter of instructions from the attorney.

12.   I. The deputy sheriff may confer with the defendant and may enter this defendants'   12.____
place of business.
     II. A deputy sheriff must ascertain from the creditor's attorney whether the debtor
has any property against which he may proceede.

13.   I. The sheriff has a right to do whatever is reasonably necessary for the purpose of   13.____
executing the order of the court.
     II. The written order of the court gives the sheriff general authority and he is gov-
erned in his acts by a very simple principal.

14.   I. Either the patrolman or his sergeant are always ready to help the public.   14.____
     II. The sergeant asked the patrolman when he would finish the report.

15.   I. The injured man could not hardly talk.   15.____
     II. Every officer had ought to hand in their reports on time.

Questions 16-25.

DIRECTIONS: For each of the sentences given below, numbered 16 through 25, select from
the following choices the MOST correct choice and print your choice in the
space at the right. Select as your answer:

    A. If the statement contains an unnecessary word or expression
    B. If the statement contains a slang term or expression ordinarily not
acceptable in government report writing
    C. If the statement contains an old-fashioned word or expression, where a
concrete, plain term would be more useful
    D. If the statement contains no major faults

16. Every one of us should try harder   16.____

17. Yours of the first instant has been received.   17.____

18. We will have to do a real snow job on him.   18.____

19. I shall contact him next Thursday.   19.____

20. None of us were invited to the meeting with the community.

21. We got this here job to do.

22. She could not help but see the mistake in the checkbook.

23. Don't bug the Director about the report.

24. I beg to inform you that your letter has been received.

25. This project is all screwed up.

20._____

21._____

22._____

23._____

24._____

25._____

KEY (CORRECT ANSWERS)

1.	D		11.	B
2.	C		12.	D
3.	A		13.	A
4.	D		14.	D
5.	B		15.	D
6.	B		16.	D
7.	A		17.	C
8.	D		18.	B
9.	D		19.	D
10.	C		20.	D

21.	B
22.	D
23.	B
24.	C
25.	B

TEST 3

DIRECTIONS: Questions 1 through 25 are sentences taken from reports. Some are correct according to ordinary formal English usage. Others are incorrect because they contain errors in English usage, spelling, or punctuation. Consider a sentence correct if it contains no errors in English usage, spelling, or punctuation, even if there may be other ways of writing the sentence correctly. Mark your answer:

    A. If only sentence I is correct
    B. If only sentence II is correct
    C. If sentences I and II are correct
    D. If neither sentence I nor II is correct.

1.   I. The Neighborhood Police Team Commander and Team Patrol- men are encour- aged to give to the public the widest possible verbal and written disemination of information regarding the existence and purposes of the program.
    II. The police must be vitally interelated with every segment of the public they serve.

    1._____

2.   I. If social gambling, prostitution, and other vices are to be prohibited, the law makers should provide the manpower and method for enforcement.
    II. In addition to checking on possible crime locations such as hallways, roofs yards and other similar locations, Team Patrolmen are encouraged to make known their presence to members of the community.

    2._____

3.   I. The Neighborhood Police Team Commander is authorized to secure, the coopera- tion of local publications, as well as public and private agencies, to further the goals of the program.
    II. Recruitment from social minorities is essential to effective police work among minorities and meaningful relations with them.

    3._____

4.   I. The Neighborhood Police Team Commander and his men have the responsibility for providing patrol service within the sector territory on a twenty-four hour basis.
    II. While the patrolman was walking his beat at midnight he noticed that the clothing stores' door was partly open.

    4._____

5.   I. Authority is granted to the Neighborhood Police Team to device tactics for coping with the crime in the sector.
    II. Before leaving the scene of the accident, the patrolman drew a map showing the positions of the automobiles and indicated the time of the accident as 10 M. in the morning.

    5._____

6.   I. The Neighborhood Police Team Commander and his men must be kept apprised of conditions effecting their sector.
    II. Clear, continuous communication with every segment of the public served based on the realization of mutual need and founded on trust and confidence is the basis for effective law enforcement.

    6._____

7.   I.   The irony is that the police are blamed for the laws they enforce when they are doing their duty.

      II.   The Neighborhood Police Team Commander is authorized to prepare and distribute literature with pertinent information telling the public whom to contact for assistance.

7.____

8.   I.   The day is not far distant when major parts of the entire police compliment will need extensive college training or degrees.

      II.   Although driving under the influence of alcohol is a specific charge in making arrests, drunkeness is basically a health and social problem.

8.____

9.   I.   If a deputy sheriff finds that property he has to attach is located on a ship, he should notify his supervisor.

      II.   Any contract that tends to interfere with the administration of justice is illegal.

9.____

10.   I.   A mandate or official order of the court to the sheriff or other officer directs it to take into possession property of the judgment debtor.

      II.   Tenancies from month-to-month, week-to-week, and sometimes year-to-year are termenable.

10.____

11.   I.   A civil arrest is an arrest pursuant to an order issued by a court in civil litigation.

      II.   In a criminal arrest, a defendant is arrested for a crime he is alleged to have committed.

11.____

12.   I.   Having taken a defendant into custody, there is a complete restraint of personal liberty.

      II.   Actual force is unnecessary when a deputy sheriff makes an arrest.

12.____

13.   I.   When a husband breaches a separation agreement by failing to supply to the wife the amount of money to be paid to her periodically under the agreement, the same legal steps may be taken to enforce his compliance as in any other breach of contract.

      II.   Having obtained the writ of attachment, the plaintiff is then in the advantageous position of selling the very property that has been held for him by the sheriff while he was obtaining a judgment.

13.____

14.   I.   Being locked in his desk, the investigator felt sure that the records would be safe.

      II.   The reason why the witness changed his statement was because he had been threatened.

14.____

15.   I.   The investigation had just began then an important witness disappeared.

      II.   The check that had been missing was located and returned to its owner, Harry Morgan, a resident of Suffolk County, New York.

15.____

16.   I.   A supervisor will find that the establishment of standard procedures enables his staff to work more efficiently.

      II.   An investigator hadn't ought to give any recommendations in his report if he is in doubt.

16.____

17.   I.   Neither the investigator nor his supervisor is ready to interview the witnesses.

      II.   Interviewing has been and always will be an important asset in investigation.

17.____

18.   I. One of the investigator's reports has been forwarded to the wrong person.   18.____
      II. The investigator stated that he was not familiar with those kind of cases.

19.   I. Approaching the victim of the assault, two large bruises were noticed by me.   19.____
      II. The prisoner was arrested for assault, resisting arrest, and use of a deadly weapon.

20.   I. A copy of the orders, which had been prepared by the captain, was given to each   20.____
patrolman.
      II. It's always necessary to inform an arrested person of his constitutional rights before asking him any questions.

21.   I. To prevent further bleeding, I applied a tourniquet to the wound.   21.____
      II. John Rano a senior officer was on duty at the time of the accident.

22.   I. Limiting the term "property" to tangible property, in the criminal mischief setting,   22.____
accords with prior case law holding that only tangible property came within the purview of the offense of malicious mischief.
      II. Thus, a person who intentionally destroys the property of another, but under an honest belief that he has title to such property, cannot be convicted of criminal mischief under the Revised Penal Law.

23.   I. Very early in it's history, New York enacted statutes from time to time punishing,   23.____
either as a felony or as a misdemeanor, malicious injuries to various kinds of property: piers, booms, dams, bridges, etc.
      II. The application of the statute is necessarily restricted to trespassory takings with larcenous intent: namely with intent permanently or virtually permanently to "appropriate" property or "deprive" the owner of its use.

24.   I. Since the former Penal Law did not define the instruments of forgery in a general   24.____
fashion, its crime of forgery was held to be narrower than the common law offense in this respect and to embrace only those instruments explicitly specified in the substantive provisions.
      II. After entering the barn through an open door for the purpose of stealing, it was closed by the defendants.

25.   I. The use of fire or explosives to destroy tangible property is proscribed by the crim-   25.____
inal mischief provisions of the Revised Penal Law.
      II. The defendant's taking of a taxicab for the immediate purpose of affecting his escape did not constitute grand larceny.

KEY (CORRECT ANSWERS)

1.	D	11.	C
2.	D	12.	B
3.	B	13.	C
4.	A	14.	D
5.	D	15.	B
6.	D	16.	A
7.	C	17.	C
8.	D	18.	A
9.	C	19.	B
10.	D	20.	C

21.	A
22.	C
23.	B
24.	A
25.	A

TEST 4

Questions 1-4.

DIRECTIONS: Each of the two sentences in Questions 1 through 4 may be correct or may contain errors in punctuation, capitalization, or grammar. Mark your answer:

A.   If there is an error only in sentence I
B.   If there is an error only in sentence II
C.   If there is an error in both sentences I and II
D.   If both sentences are correct.

1.   I.   It is very annoying to have a pencil sharpener, which is not in working order.   1.____
     II. Patrolman Blake checked the door of Joe's Restaurant and found that the lock has been jammed.

2.   I.   When you are studying a good textbook is important.   2.____
     II. He said he would divide the money equally between you and me.

3.   I.   Since he went on the city council a year ago, one of his primary concerns has been safety in the streets.   3.____
     II. After waiting in the doorway for about 15 minutes, a black sedan appeared.

Questions 5-9.

DIRECTIONS: Each of the sentences in Questions 5 through 9 may be classified under one of the following four categories:
A.   Faulty because of incorrect grammar
B.   Faulty because of incorrect punctuation
C.   Faulty because of incorrect capitalization or incorrect spelling
D.   Correct

Examine each sentence carefully to determine under which of the above four options it is BEST classified. Then, in the space at the right, print the capital-ized letter preceding the option which is the BEST of the four suggested above. Each faulty sentence contains but one type of error. Consider a sen-tence to be correct if it contains none of the types of errors mentioned, even though there may be other correct ways of expressing the same thought.

5.   They told both he and I that the prisoner had escaped.   5.____

6.   Any superior officer, who, disregards the just complaints of his subordinates, is remiss in the performance of his duty.   6.____

7.   Only those members of the national organization who resided in the Middle west attended the conference in Chicago.   7.____

8.   We told him to give the investigation assignment to whoever was available.   8.____

9.   Please do not disappoint and embarass us by not appearing in court.   9.____

Questions 10-14.

DIRECTIONS: Each of Questions 10 through 14 consists of three sentences lettered A, B, and C. In each of these questions, one of the sentences may contain an error in grammar, sentence structure, or punctuation, or all three sentences may be correct. If one of the sentences in a question contains an error in grammar, sentence structure, or punctuation, print in the space at the right the capital letter preceding the sentence which contains the error. If all three sentences are correct, print the letter D.

10. A. Mr. Smith appears to be less competent than I in performing these duties.   10._____
      B. The supervisor spoke to the employee, who had made the error, but did not reprimand him.
      C. When he found the book lying on the table, he immediately notified the owner.

11. A. Being locked in the desk, we were certain that the papers would not be taken.   11._____
      B. It wasn't I who dictated the telegram; I believe it was Eleanor.
      C. You should interview whoever comes to the office today.

12. A. The clerk was instructed to set the machine on the table before summoning the manager.   12._____
      B. He said that he was not familiar with those kind of activities.
      C. A box of pencils, in addition to erasers and blotters, was included in the shipment of supplies.

13. A. The supervisor remarked, "Assigning an employee to the proper type of work is not always easy."   13._____
      B. The employer found that each of the applicants were qualified to perform the duties of the position.
      C. Any competent student is permitted to take this course if he obtains the consent of the instructor.

14. A. The prize was awarded to the employee whom the judges believed to be most deserving.   14._____
      B. Since the instructor believes this book is the better of the two, he is recommending it for use in the school.
      C. It was obvious to the employees that the completion of the task by the scheduled date would require their working overtime.

Questions 15-21.

DIRECTIONS: In answering Questions 15 through 21, choose the sentence which is BEST from the point of view of English usage suitable for a business report.

15. A. The client's receiving of public assistance checks at two different addresses were disclosed by the investigation.
    B. The investigation disclosed that the client was receiving public assistance checks at two different addresses.
    C. The client was found out by the investigation to be receiving public assistance checks at two different addresses.
    D. The client has been receiving public assistance checks at two different addresses, disclosed the investigation.

15.____

16. A. The investigation of complaints are usually handled by this unit, which deals with internal security problems in the department.
    B. This unit deals with internal security problems in the department usually investigating complaints.
    C. Investigating complaints is this unit's job, being that it handles internal security problems in the department.
    D. This unit deals with internal security problems in the department and usually investigates complaints.

16.____

17. A. The delay in completing this investigation was caused by difficulty in obtaining the required documents from the candidate.
    B. Because of difficulty in obtaining the required documents from the candidate is the reason that there was a delay in completing this investigation.
    C. Having had difficulty in obtaining the required documents from the candidate, there was a delay in completing this investigation.
    D. Difficulty in obtaining the required documents from the candidate had the affect of delaying the completion of this investigation.

17.____

18. A. This report, together with documents supporting our recommendation, are being submitted for your approval.
    B. Documents supporting our recommendation is being submitted with the report for your approval.
    C. This report, together with documents supporting our recommendation, is being submitted for your approval.
    D. The report and documents supporting our recommendation is being submitted for your approval.

18.____

19. A. The chairman himself, rather than his aides, has reviewed the report.
    B. The chairman himself, rather than his aides, have reviewed the report.
    C. The chairmen, not the aide, has reviewed the report.
    D. The aide, not the chairmen, have reviewed the report.

19.____

20. A. Various proposals were submitted but the decision is not been made.
    B. Various proposals has been submitted but the decision has not been made.
    C. Various proposals were submitted but the decision is not been made.
    D. Various proposals have been submitted but the decision has not been made.

20.____

21. A. Everyone were rewarded for his successful attempt.
    B. They were successful in their attempts and each of them was rewarded.
    C. Each of them are rewarded for their successful attempts.
    D. The reward for their successful attempts were made to each of them.

21.____

22. The following is a paragraph from a request for departmental recognition consisting of   22._____
five numbered sentences submitted to a Captain for review. These sentences may or
may not have errors in spelling, grammar, and punctuation:

1. The officers observed the subject Mills surreptitiously remove a wallet from the
woman's handbag and entered his automobile. 2. As they approached Mills, he looked in
their direction and drove away. 3. The officers pursued in their car. 4. Mills executed a
series of complicated manuvers to evade the pursuing officers. 5. At the corner of
Broome and Elizabeth Streets, Mills stopped the car, got out, raised his hands and sur-
rendered to the officers.

Which one of the following BEST classifies the above with regard to spelling, grammar
and punctuation?

   A.   1, 2, and 3 are correct, but 4 and 5 have errors.
   B.   2, 3, and 5 are correct, but 1 and 4 have errors.
   C.   3, 4, and 5 are correct, but 1 and 2 have errors.
   D.   1, 2, 3, and 5 are correct, but 4 has errors.

23. The one of the following sentences which is grammatically PREFERABLE to the others   23._____
is:

   A.   Our engineers will go over your blueprints so that you may have no problems in
        construction.
   B.   For a long time he had been arguing that we, not he, are to blame for the confu-
        sion.
   C.   I worked on this automobile for two hours and still cannot find out what is wrong
        with it.
   D.   Accustomed to all kinds of hardships, fatigue seldom bothers veteran policemen.

24. The MOST accurate of the following sentences is: 24._____

   A.   The commissioner, as well as his deputy and various bureau heads, were present.
   B.   A new organization of employers and employees have been formed.
   C.   One or the other of these men have been selected.
   D.   The number of pages in the book is enough to discourage a reader.

25. The MOST accurate of the following sentences is: 25._____

   A.   Between you and me, I think he is the better man.
   B.   He was believed to be me.
   C.   Is it us that you wish to see?
   D.   The winners are him and her.

KEY (CORRECT ANSWERS)

1.	C	11.	A
2.	A	12.	B
3.	C	13.	B
4.	B	14.	D
5.	A	15.	B
6.	B	16.	D
7.	C	17.	A
8.	D	18.	C
9.	C	19.	A
10.	B	20.	D
		21.	B
		22.	B
		23.	A
		24.	D
		25.	A

READING COMPREHENSION
UNDERSTANDING AND INTERPRETING WRITTEN MATERIAL
EXAMINATION SECTION
TEST 1

DIRECTIONS: Each question or incomplete statement is followed by several suggested answers or completions. Select the one that BEST answers the question or completes the statement. *PRINT THE LETTER OF THE CORRECT ANSWER IN THE SPACE AT THE RIGHT.*

Questions 1-2.

DIRECTIONS: Questions 1 and 2 are to be answered SOLELY on the basis of the information given in the following paragraph .

It is argued by some that the locale of the trial should be given little or no consideration. Facts are facts, they say, and if presented properly to a jury panel they will be productive of the same results regardless of where the trial is held. However, experience shows great differences in the methods of handling claims by juries. In some counties, large demands in personal injury suits are viewed with suspicion by the jury. In others, the jurors are liberal in dealing with someone else's funds.

1. According to the above paragraph, it would be ADVISABLE for an examiner on a personal injury case to   1.____

    A. get information as to the kind of verdicts that are usually awarded by juries in the county of trial
    B. give little or no consideration to the locale of the trial
    C. look for incomplete and improper presentation of facts to the jury if the verdict was not justified by the facts
    D. offer a high but realistic initial settlement figure so that no temptation is left to the claimant to gamble on the jury's verdict

2. According to the above statement, the argument that the location of a trial in a personal injury suit CANNOT counteract the weight of the evidence is   2.____

    A. basically sound
    B. disproven by the differences in awards for similar claims
    C. substantiated in those cases where the facts are properly and carefully presented to the injury
    D. supported by experience which shows great differences in the methods of handling claims by juries

Questions 3-6.

DIRECTIONS: Questions 3 through 6 are to be answered SOLELY on the basis of the following excerpt from a recorded annual report of the police department. This material should be read first and then referred to in answering these questions.

LEGAL BUREAU

One of the more important functions of this bureau is to analyze and furnish the department with pertinent information concerning Federal and State statutes and local laws which affect the department, law enforcement or crime prevention. In addition, all measure introduced in the State Legislature and the City Council which may affect this department are carefully reviewed by members of the Legal Bureau and, where necessary, opinions and recommendations thereon are prepared.

Another important function of this office is the prosecution of cases in the Criminal Courts. This is accomplished by assignment of attorneys who are members of the Legal Bureau to appear in those cases which are deemed to raise issues of importance to the department or questions of law which require technical presentation to facilitate proper determination; and also in those cases where request is made for such appearances by a judge or magistrate, some other official of the city, or a member of the force.

Proposed legislation was prepared and sponsored for introduction in the State Legislature and, at this writing, one of these proposals has already been enacted into law and five others are presently on the Governor's desk awaiting executive action. The new law prohibits the sale or possession of a hypodermic syringe or needle by an unauthorized person. The bureau's proposals awaiting executive action pertain to an amendment to the Criminal Procedure Law prohibiting desk officers from taking bail in gambling cases or in cases mentioned in the Criminal Procedure Law, including confidence men and swindlers as jostlers in the Penal Law; prohibiting the sale of switchblade knives of any size to children under 16 and bills extending the licensing period of gunsmiths.

The Legal Bureau has regularly cooperated with the Corporation Counsel and the District Attorneys in respect to matters affecting this department, and has continued to advise and represent the Police Athletic League, the Police Sports Association, the Police Relief Fund, and the Police Pension Fund.

3. Members of the Legal Bureau frequently appear in Criminal Court for the purpose of   3.____

   A. defending members of the Police Force
   B. raising issues of important to the Police Department
   C. prosecuting all offenders arrested by members of the Force
   D. facilitating proper determination of questions of law requiring technical presentation

4. The Legal Bureau sponsored a bill that would   4.____

   A. extend the licenses of gunsmiths
   B. prohibit the sale of switchblade knives to children of any size
   C. place confidence men and swindlers in the same category as jostlers in the Penal Law
   D. prohibit desk officers from admitting gamblers, confidence men, and swindlers to bail

5. One of the functions of the Legal Bureau is to   5.____

     A. review and make recommendations on proposed Federal laws affecting law enforcement
     B. prepare opinions on all measures introduced in the State Legislature and the City Council
     C. furnish the Police Department with pertinent information concerning all new Federal and State laws
     D. analyze all laws affecting the work of the Police Department

6. The one of the following that is NOT a function of the Legal Bureau is   6.____

     A. law enforcement and crime prevention
     B. prosecution of all cases in Women's Court
     C. advise and represent the Police Sports Association
     D. lecturing at the Police Academy

7. It is usual in public service for recruits to serve a probationary period before they receive   7.____
tenured positions. The objective of this is to observe them in actual service, to teach them the duties of their position, and to provide a means for eliminating those who prove they are not suited for this kind of work. During this period, firings may be made at the discretion of the chief.
Which one of the following is BEST supported by the above selection?

     A. Demonstrated fitness for the job is the basis for retention of probationary employees.
     B. Trial appointments protect the appointee from unfair dismissal practices.
     C. Public service employees need experience and instruction before permanent appointment.
     D. Exams must be given to determine the ability of probationary employees.

8. As the fundamental changes sought to be brought about in the inmates of a correctional   8.____
institution can be accomplished only under good leadership, it follows that the quality of the staff whose duty it is to influence and guide the inmates in the right direction is more important than the physical facilities of the institution.
Of the following, the MOST accurate conclusion based on the preceding statement is that

     A. the development of leadership is the fundamental change brought about in inmates by good quality staff
     B. the physical facilities of an institution are not very important in bringing about fundamental changes in the inmates
     C. with proper training the entire staff of a correctional institution can be developed into good leaders
     D. without good leadership the basic changes desired in the inmates of a correctional institution cannot be brought about

Questions 9-11.

DIRECTIONS: Questions 9 through 11 are to be answered SOLELY on the basis of the following paragraph.

The law enforcement agency is one of the most important agencies in the field of juvenile delinquency prevention. This is so not because of the social work connected with this problem, however, for this is not a police matter, but because the officers are usually the first to come in contact with the delinquent. The manner of arrest and detention makes a deep impression upon him and affects his life-long attitude toward society and the law. The juvenile court is perhaps the most important agency in this work. Contrary to the general opinion, however, it is not primarily concerned with putting children into correctional schools. The main purpose of the juvenile court is to save the child and to develop his emotional make-up in order that he can grow up to be a decent and well-balanced citizen. The system of probation is the means whereby the court seeks to accomplish these goals.

9. According to this paragraph, police work is an important part of a program to prevent juvenile delinquency because 9.____

    A. social work is no longer considered important in juvenile delinquency prevention
    B. police officers are the first to have contact with the delinquent
    C. police officers jail the offender in order to be able to change his attitude toward society and the law
    D. it is the first step in placing the delinquent in jail

10. According to this paragraph, the CHIEF purpose of the juvenile court is to 10.____

    A. punish the child for his offense
    B. select a suitable correctional school for the delinquent
    C. use available means to help the delinquent become a better person
    D. provide psychiatric care for the delinquent

11. According to this paragraph, the juvenile court directs the development of delinquents under its care CHIEFLY by 11.____

    A. placing the child under probation
    B. sending the child to a correctional school
    C. keeping the delinquent in prison
    D. returning the child to his home

Questions 12-14.

DIRECTIONS: Questions 12 through 14 are to be answered on the basis of the following paragraph.

An assassination is an act that consists of a plotted, attempted or actual murder of a prominent political figure by an individual who performs this act in other than a governmental role. This definition draws a distinction between political execution and assassination. An execution may be regarded as a political killing, but it is initiated by the organs of the state, while an assassination can always be characterized as an illegal act. A prominent figure must be the target of the killing, since the killing of lesser members of the political community is included within a wider category of internal political turmoil, namely, terrorism. Assassination is also to be distinguished from homicide. The target of the aggressive act must be a political figure rather than a private person. The killing of a prime minister by a member of an insurrectionist or underground group clearly qualifies as an assassination. So does an act by a deranged individual who tries to kill not just any individual, but the individual in his political role - as President, for example.

12. Assume that a nationally prominent political figure is charged with treason by the state, tried in a court of law, found guilty, and hanged by the state. According to the above passage, it would be MOST appropriate to regard his death as a(n)

    A. assassination
    B. execution
    C. aggressive act
    D. homicide

12.____

13. According to the above passage, which of the following statements is CORRECT?

    A. The assassination of a political figure is an illegal act.
    B. A private person may be the target of an assassination attempt.
    C. The killing of an obscure member of a political community is considered an assassination event.
    D. An execution may not be regarded as a political killing.

13.____

14. Of the following, the MOST appropriate title for this passage would be

    A. ASSASSINATION - LEGAL ASPECTS
    B. POLITICAL CAUSES OF ASSASSINATION
    C. ASSASSINATION - A DEFINITION
    D. CATEGORIES OF ASSASSINATION

14.____

Questions 15-17.

DIRECTIONS: Questions 15 through 17 are to be answered SOLELY on the basis of the following paragraph.

All applicants for an original license to operate a catering establishment shall be fingerprinted. This shall include the officers, employees, and stockholders of the company and the members of a partnership. In case of a change, by addition or substitution, occurring during the existence of a license, the person added or substituted shall be fingerprinted. However, in the case of a hotel containing more than 200 rooms, only the officer or manager filing the application is required to be fingerprinted. The police commissioner may also, at his discretion, exempt the employees and stockholders of any company. The fingerprints shall be taken on one copy of Form C.E. 20 and on two copies of C.E. 21. One copy of Form C.E. 21 shall accompany the application. Fingerprints are not required with a renewal application.

15. According to the above paragraph, an employee added to the payroll of a licensed catering establishment which is not in a hotel must be fingerprinted

    A. always
    B. unless he has been previously fingerprinted for another license
    C. unless exempted by the police commissioner
    D. only if he is the manager or an officer of the company

15.____

16. According to the above paragraph, it would be MOST accurate to state that

    A. Form C.E. 20 must accompany a renewal application
    B. Form C.E. 21 must accompany all applications
    C. Form C.E. 21 must accompany an original application
    D. both Forms C.E. 20 and C.E. 21 must accompany all applications

16.____

17. A hotel of 270 rooms has applied for a license to operate a catering establishment on the premises.
According to the instructions for fingerprinting given in the above paragraph, the _____ shall be fingerprinted.

    A. officers, employees, and stockholders
    B. officers and the manager
    C. employees
    D. officer filing the application

17.____

Questions 18-24.

DIRECTIONS: Read the following two paragraphs. Then answer the questions by selecting the answer
           A - if the paragraphs indicate it is TRUE
           B - if the paragraphs indicate it is PROBABLY true
           C - if the paragraphs indicate it is PROBABLY false
           D - if the paragraphs indicate it is FALSE

The fallacy underlying what some might call the eighteenth and nineteenth century misconceptions of the nature of scientific investigations seems to lie in a mistaken analogy. Those who said they were investigating the structure of the universe imagined themselves as the equivalent of the early explorers and map makers. The explorers of the fifteenth and sixteenth centuries had opened up new worlds with the aid of imperfect maps; in their accounts of distant lands, there had been some false and many ambiguous statements. But by the time everyone came to believe the world was round, the maps of distant continents were beginning to assume a fairly consistent pattern. By the seventeenth century, methods of measuring space and time had laid the foundations for an accurate geography.

On this basic issue there is far from complete agreement among philosophers *of* science today. You can, each of you, choose your side and find highly distinguished advocates for the point of view you have selected. However, in view of the revolution in physics, anyone who now asserts that science is an exploration of the universe must be prepared to shoulder a heavy burden of proof. To my mind, the analogy between the map maker and the scientist is false. A scientific theory is not even the first approximation to a map; it is not a need; it is a policy -- an economical and fruitful guide to action, by scientific investigators.

18. The author thinks that 18th and 19th century science followed the same technique as the 15th century geographers.

18.____

19. The author disagrees with the philosophers who are labelled realists.

19.____

20. The author believes there is a permanent structure to the universe.

20.____

21. A scientific theory is an economical guide to exploring what cannot be known absolutely.

21.____

22. Philosophers of science accept the relativity implications of recent research in physics.

22.____

23. It is a matter of time and effort before modern scientists will be as successful as the geographers.

23.____

24. The author believes in an indeterminate universe.

24.____

25. Borough X reports that its police force makes fewer arrests per thousand persons than any of the other boroughs. 25.____
    From this statement, it is MOST probable that

    A. sufficient information has not been given to warrant any conclusion
    B. the police force of Borough X is less efficient
    C. fewer crimes are being committed in Borough X
    D. fewer crimes are being reported in Borough X

KEY (CORRECT ANSWERS)

1.	A		11.	A
2.	B		12.	B
3.	D		13.	A
4.	C		14.	C
5.	D		15.	C
6.	A		16.	C
7.	A		17.	D
8.	D		18.	D
9.	B		19.	B
10.	C		20.	D

21.	A
22.	D
23.	D
24.	B
25.	A

TEST 2

DIRECTIONS: Each question or incomplete statement is followed by several suggested answers or completions. Select the one that BEST answers the question or completes the statement. *PRINT THE LETTER OF THE CORRECT ANSWER IN THE SPACE AT THE RIGHT.*

Questions 1-2.

DIRECTIONS: Questions 1 and 2 are to be answered on the basis of the information given in the following passage.

Assume that a certain agency is having a problem at one of its work locations because a sizable portion of the staff at that location is regularly tardy in reporting to work. The management of the agency is primarily concerned about eliminating the problem and is not yet too concerned about taking any disciplinary action. An investigator is assigned to investigate to determine, if possible, what might be causing this problem.

After several interviews, the investigator sees that low morale created by poor supervision at this location is at least part of the problem. In addition, there is a problem of tardiness and lack of interest.

1. Given the goals of the investigation and assuming that the investigator was using a non-directive approach in this interview, of the following, the investigator's MOST effective response should be:

    A.   You know, you are building a bad record of tardiness
    B.   Can you tell me more about this situation?
    C.   What kind of person is your superior?
    D.   Do you think you are acting fairly towards the agency by being late so often?

1.____

2. Given the goals of the investigation and assuming the investigator was using a directed approach in this interview, of the following, the investigator's response should be:

    A.   That doesn't seem like much of an excuse to me
    B.   What do you mean by saying that you've lost interest?
    C.   What problems are there with the supervision you are getting?
    D.   How do you think your tardiness looks in your personnel record?

2.____

Questions 3-5.

DIRECTIONS: Questions 3 through 5 are to be answered SOLELY on the basis of the following passage.

As investigators, we are more concerned with the utilitarian than the philosophical aspects of ethics and ethical standards, procedures, and conduct. As a working consideration, we might view ethics as the science of doing the right thing at the right time in the right manner in conformity with the normal, everyday standards imposed by society; and in conformity with the judgment society would be expected to make concerning the rightness or wrongness of what we have done.

An ethical code might be considered a basic set of rules and regulations to which we must conform in the performance of investigative duties. Ethical standards, procedures, and conduct might be considered the logical workings of our ethical code in its everyday application to our work. Ethics also necessarily involves morals and morality. We must eventually answer the self-imposed question of whether or not we have acted in the right way in conducting our investigative activities in their individual and total aspects.

3. Of the following, the MOST suitable title for the above passage is

3.____

    A. THE IMPORTANCE OF RULES FOR INVESTIGATORS
    B. THE BASIC PHILOSOPHY OF A LAWFUL SOCIETY
    C. SCIENTIFIC ASPECTS OF INVESTIGATIONS
    D. ETHICAL GUIDELINES FOR THE CONDUCT OF INVESTIGATIONS

4. According to the above passage, ethical considerations for investigators involve

4.____

    A. special standards that are different from those which apply to the rest of society
    B. practices and procedures which cannot be evaluated by others
    C. individual judgments by investigators of the appropriateness of their own actions
    D. regulations which are based primarily upon a philosophical approach

5. Of the following, the author's PRINCIPAL purpose in writing the above passage seems to have been to

5.____

    A. emphasize the importance of self-criticism in investigative activities
    B. explain the relationship that exists between ethics and investigative conduct
    C. reduce the amount of unethical conduct in the area of investigations
    D. seek recognition by his fellow investigators for his academic treatment of the subject matter

Questions 6-8.

DIRECTIONS: Questions 6 through 8 are to be answered SOLELY on the basis of the following passage.

The investigator must remember that acts of omission can be as effective as acts of commission in affecting the determination of disputed issues. Acts of omission, such as failure to obtain available information or failure to verify dubious information, manifest themselves in miscarriages of justice and erroneous adjudications. An incomplete investigation is an erroneous investigation because a conclusion predicated upon inadequate facts is based on quicksand.

When an investigator throws up his hands and admits defeat, the reason for this action does not necessarily lie in his possible laziness and ineptitude. It is more likely that the investigator has made his conclusions after exhausting only those avenues of investigation of which he is aware. He has exercised good faith in his belief that nothing else can be done.

This tendency must be overcome by all investigators if they are to operate at top efficiency. If no suggestion for new or additional action can be found in any authority, an investigator should use his own initiative to cope with a given situation. No investigator should ever hesitate to set precedents. It is far better in the final analysis to attempt difficult solutions, even if the chances of error are obviously present, than it is to take refuge in the spineless adage: If you don't do anything, you don't do it wrong.

6. Of the following, the MOST suitable title for the above passage is   6.____

    A. THE NEED FOR RESOURCEFULNESS IN INVESTIGATIONS
    B. PROCEDURES FOR COMPLETING AN INVESTIGATION
    C. THE DEVELOPMENT OF STANDARDS FOR INVESTIGATORS
    D. THE CAUSES OF INCOMPLETE INVESTIGATIONS

7. Of the following, the author of this passage considers that the LEAST important consid-   7.____
eration in developing new investigative methods is

    A. efficiency   B. caution
    C. imagination   D. thoroughness

8. According to this passage, which of the following statements is INCORRECT?   8.____

    A. Lack of creativity may lead to erroneous investigations .
    B. Acts of omission are sometimes as harmful as acts of commission.
    C. Some investigators who give up on a case are lazy or inept.
    D. An investigator who gives up on a case is usually not acting in good faith.

Questions 9-12.

DIRECTIONS: Questions 9 through 12 are to be answered on the basis of the following para-
                 graph.

A report of investigation should not be weighed down by a mass of information which is
hardly material or only remotely relevant, or which fails to prove a point, clarify an issue, or aid
the inquiry even by indirection. Some investigative agencies, however, value the report for its
own sake, considering it primarily as a justification of the investigative activity contained
therein. Every step is listed to show that no logical measure has been overlooked and to
demonstrate that the reporting agent is beyond criticism. This system serves to provide
reviewing authorities with a ready means of checking subordinates and provides order,
method, and routine to investigative activity. In addition, it may offer supervisors and investigators a sense of security; the investigator would know within fairly exact limits what is
expected of him and the supervisor may be comforted by the knowledge that his organization
may not be reasonably criticized in a particular case on the grounds of obvious omissions or
inertia. To the state's attorney and others, however, who must take administrative action on
the basis of the report, the irrelevant and immaterial information thwarts the purpose of the
investigation by dimming the issues and obscuring the facts that are truly contributory to the
proof.

9. From the point of view of the supervising investigator, a drawback of having the investiga-   9.____
tor prepare the type of report which the state's attorney would like is that it

    A. gives a biased and one-sided view of what should have been an impartial investi-
        gation
    B. has only limited usefulness as an indication that all proper investigative methods
        were used by the investigator
    C. overlooks logical measures, removing the responsibility for taking those measures
        which the investigator should otherwise have been expected to take
    D. sets fairly exact limits to what the supervisor can expect of the investigator

10. District attorneys do not like reports of investigations in which every step is listed because   10.____

    A. their administrative action is then based on irrelevant and immaterial information
    B. it places the investigator beyond criticism, making the responsibility of the district attorney that much greater
    C. of the difficulty of finding among the mass of information the portion which is meaningful and useful
    D. the inclusion of indirect or hardly material information is not in accord with the order in which the steps were taken

11. As expressed in the above paragraph, the type of report which MOST investigators prefer to prepare is   11.____

    A. a step-by-step account of their activities, including both fruitful and unfruitful steps, since to do so provides order and method and gives them a sense of security
    B. not made clear, even though current practice in some agencies is to include every step taken in the investigation
    C. one from which useless and confusing information has been excluded because it is not helpful and is poor practice
    D. one not weighed down by a mass of irrelevant information but one which shows within fairly exact limits what was expected of them

12. With regard to the type of information which an investigator should include in his report, the above paragraph expresses the opinion that   12.____

    A. it is best to include in the report only that information which supports the conclusions of the investigator
    B. reports should include all relevant and clarifying information and exclude information on inquiries which had no productive result
    C. reports should include sufficient information to demonstrate that the investigator has been properly attending to his duties and all the information which contributes toward proof of what occurred in the case
    D. the most logical thing to do is to list every step in the investigation and its result

Questions 13-17.

DIRECTIONS: Questions 13 through 17 are to be answered SOLELY on the basis of the following paragraph.

Those statutes of limitations which are of interest to a claim examiner are the ones affecting third party actions brought against an insured covered by a liability policy of insurance. Such statutes of limitations are legislative enactments limiting the time within which such actions at law may be brought. Research shows that such periods differ from state to state and vary within the states with the type of action brought. The laws of the jurisdiction in which the action is brought govern and determine the period within which the action may be instituted, regardless of the place of the cause of action or the residence of the parties at the time of cause of action. The period of time set by a statute of limitations for a tort action starts from the moment the alleged tort is committed. The period usually extends continuously until its expiration, upon which legal action may no longer be brought. However, there is a suspension of the running of the period when a defendant has concealed himself in order to avoid service of legal process. The suspension continues until the defendant discontinues his concealment and then the period starts running again. A defendant may, by his agreement or conduct, be legally barred from asserting the statute of limitations as a defense to an action. The insurance carrier for the defendant may, by the misrepresentation of the claims man, cause such a bar against use of the statute of limitations by the defendant. If the claim examiner of the insurance carrier has by his conduct or assertion lulled the plaintiff into a false sense of security by false representations, the defendant may be barred from setting up the statute of limitations as a defense.

13. Of the following, the MOST suitable title for the above paragraph is 13.____

    A. FRAUDULENT USE OF THE STATUTE OF LIMITATIONS
    B. PARTIES AT INTEREST IN A LAWSUIT
    C. THE CLAIM EXAMINER AND THE LAW
    D. THE STATUTE OF LIMITATIONS IN CLAIMS WORK

14. The period of time during which a third party action may be brought against an insured covered by a liability policy depends on 14.____

    A. the laws of the jurisdiction in which the action is brought
    B. where the cause of action which is the subject of the suit took place
    C. where the claimant lived at the time of the cause of action
    D. where the insured lived at the time of the cause of action

15. Time limits in third party actions which are set by the statutes of limitations described above are 15.____

    A. determined by claimant's place of residence at start of action
    B. different in a state for different actions
    C. the same from state to state for the same type of action
    D. the same within a state regardless of type of action

16. According to the above paragraph, grounds which may be legally used to prevent a defendant from using the statute of limitations as a defense in the action described are 16.____

    A. defendant's agreement or concealment; a charge of liability for death and injury
    B. defendant's agreement or conduct; misrepresentation by the claims man
    C. fraudulent concealment by claim examiner; a charge of liability for death or injury; defendant's agreement
    D. misrepresentation by claim examiner of carrier; defendant's agreement; plaintiff's concealment

17. Suppose an alleged tort was commited on January 1, 2008 and that the period in which action may be taken is set at three years by the statute of limitations. Suppose further that the defendant, in order to avoid service of legal process, had concealed himself from July 1, 2010 through December 31, 2010.
In this case, the defendant may not use the statute of limitations as a defense unless action is brought by the plaintiff after _____, 2011. 17.____

    A. January 1   B. February 28
    C. June 30   D. August 1

Questions 18-20.

DIRECTIONS: Questions 18 through 20 are to be answered SOLELY on the basis of information contained in the following passage.

No matter how well the interrogator adjusts himself to the witness and how precisely he induces the witness to describe his observations, mistakes still can be made. The mistakes made by an experienced interrogator may be comparatively few, but as far as the witness is concerned, his path is full of pitfalls. Modern *witness psychology* has shown that even the most honest and trustworthy witnesses are apt to make grave mistakes in good faith. It is, therefore, necessary that the interrogator get an idea of the weak links in the testimony in order to check up on them in the event that something appears to be strange or not quite satisfactory.

Unfortunately, modern witness psychology does not yet offer any means of directly testing the credibility of testimony. It lacks precision and method, in spite of worthwhile attempts on the part of learned men. At the same time, witness psychology, through the gathering of many experiences concerning the weaknesses of human testimony, has been of invaluable service. It shows clearly that only evidence of a technical nature has absolute value as proof.

Testimony may be separated into the following stages: (1) perception, (2) observation, (3) mind fixation of the observed occurrences, in which fantasy, association of ideas, and personal judgment participate, and (4) expression in oral or written form, where the testimony is transferred from one witness to another or to the interrogator.

Each of these stages offers innumerable possibilities for the distortion of testimony.

18.   The above passage indicates that having witnesses talk to each other before testifying is a practice which is GENERALLY   18.____

    A.   *desirable,* since the witnesses will be able to correct each other's errors in observation before testimony
    B.   *undesirable,* since the witnesses will collaborate on one story to tell the investigator
    C.   *undesirable,* since one witness may distort his testimony because of what another witness may erroneously say
    D.   *desirable,* since witnesses will become aware of discrepancies in their own testimony and can point out the discrepancies to the investigator

19.   According to the above passage, the one of the following which would be the MOST reliable for use as evidence would be the testimony of a   19.____

    A.   handwriting expert about a signature on a forged check
    B.   trained police officer about the identity of a criminal
    C.   laboratory technician about an accident he has observed
    D.   psychologist who has interviewed any witnesses who relate conflicting stories

20.   Concerning the validity of evidence, it is CLEAR from the above passage that   20.____

    A.   only evidence of a technical nature is at all valuable
    B.   the testimony of witnesses is so flawed that it is usually valueless

C. an investigator, by knowing modern witness psychology, will usually be able to perceive mistaken testimony
D. an investigator ought to expect mistakes in even the most reliable witness testimony

Questions 21-22.

DIRECTIONS: Questions 21 and 22 are to be answered SOLELY on the basis of the information contained in the passage below. This passage represents a report prepared by a subordinate superior concerning a school demonstration.

On April 1, a group of students, each holding an anti-apartheid sign, was involved in a demonstration on the grounds of Columbia University. The students began by locking the main entrance doors to the Administration Building and preventing faculty and students from entering or leaving the building.

The C.O. of the police detail at the scene requested additional assistance of four female detectives, an Emergency Service van, and a police photographer equipped with a Polaroid instamatic camera.

When the additional assistance arrived, the Commanding Officer directed the students to disperse. His justification for the order was that the demonstrators were violating the rights of other students and certain faculty members by denying them access to the Administration Building. The students ignored the order to disperse and the Commanding Officer of the police detail ordered them to be removed.

Another group of students who had been standing in front of the library were sympathetic toward the demonstrators and charged the police. Several police officers were injured during the ensuing hostilities.

Eventually, order was restored. That evening, the television coverage presented a neutral and fairly accurate account of the incident.

21. Which of the following statements MOST clearly and accurately reflects the contents of the report?   21.____

    A. A large group of students, all of whom were holding anti-apartheid signs, was involved in a demonstration on the grounds of Columbia University.
    B. A large group of students, some of whom were holding anti-apartheid signs, was involved in a demonstration on the grounds of Columbia University.
    C. Each of a group of Columbia students carrying anti-apartheid signs was involved in a demonstration on the grounds of Columbia University.
    D. Each of the students involved in the demonstration on the grounds of Columbia University was holding an anti-apartheid sign.

22. Which of the following statements MOST clearly and accurately reflects the contents of the report?   22.____

A. The Commanding Officer of the police detail justified his order that the demonstrators disperse when the additional assistance arrived.
B. When the additional assistance arrived, the Commanding Officer of the police detail justified his order that the demonstrators disperse.
C. The Commanding Officer of the police detail directed the students to disperse when the additional assistance arrived.
D. The Commanding Officer of the police detail requested additional assistance because the student demonstrators were violating the rights of other students and certain faculty members.

23. Which of the following statements MOST clearly and accurately reflects the contents of the report?   23.____

A. Another group of students charged the police because they were sympathetic toward the police.
B. The evening television coverage of the demonstration was fair and accurate.
C. The group of students who had been standing in front of the library was sympathetic toward the demonstrators.
D. Several police officers were injured during the hostilities which took place in front of the library.

Questions 24-25.

DIRECTIONS: Questions 24 and 25 are to be answered SOLELY on the basis of the information given in the following paragraph.

Credibility of a witness is usually governed by his character and is evidenced by his reputation for truthfulness. Personal or financial reasons or a criminal record may cause a witness to give false information to avoid being implicated. Age, sex, physical and mental abnormalities, loyalty, revenge, social and economic status, indulgence in alcohol, and the influence of other persons are some of the many factors which may affect the accuracy, willingness, or ability with which witnesses observe, interpret, and describe occurrences.

24. According to the above paragraph, a witness may, for personal reasons, give wrong information about an occurrence because he   24.____

A. wants to protect his reputation for truthfulness
B. wants to embarrass the investigator
C. doesn't want to become involved
D. doesn't really remember what happened

25. According to the above paragraph, factors which influence the witness of an occurrence may affect   25.____

A. not only what he tells about it but what he was able and wanted to see of it
B. only what he describes and interprets later but not what he actually sees at the time of the event
C. what he sees but not what he describes
D. what he is willing to see but not what he is able to see

KEY (CORRECT ANSWERS)

1.	B		11.	B
2.	C		12.	B
3.	D		13.	D
4.	C		14.	A
5.	B		15.	B
6.	A		16.	B
7.	B		17.	C
8.	D		18.	C
9.	B		19.	A
10.	C		20.	D

21.	D
22.	C
23.	C
24.	C
25.	A

EXAMINATION SECTION
TEST 1

DIRECTIONS: Each question or incomplete statement is followed by several suggested answers or completions. Select the one that *BEST* answer the question or completes the statement. *PRINT THE LETTER OF THE CORRECT ANSWER IN THE SPACE AT THE RIGHT.*

1. Although some kinds of instructions are best put in written form, a supervisor can give many instructions verbally.
   In which one of the following situations would verbal instructions be *MOST* suitable?

   A. Furnishing an employee with the details to be checked in doing a certain job
   B. Instructing an employee on the changes necessary to update the office manual used in your unit
   C. Informing a new employee where different kinds of supplies and equipment that he might need are kept
   D. Presenting an assignment to an employee who will be held accountable for following a series of steps

   1.____

2. You may be asked to evaluate the organization structure of your unit.
   Which one of the following questions would you *NOT* expect to take up in an evaluation of this kind?

   A. Is there an employee whose personal problems are interfering with his or her work?
   B. Is there an up-to-date job description for each position in this section?
   C. Are related operations and tasks grouped together and regularly assigned together?
   D. Are responsibilities divided as far as possible, and. is this division clearly understood by all employees?

   2.____

3. In order to distribute and schedule work fairly and efficiently, a supervisor may wish to make a work distribution study. A simple way of getting the information necessary for such a study is to have everyone for one week keep track of each task done and the time spent on each.
   Which one of the following situations showing up in such a study would *most clearly* call for corrective action?

   A. The newest employee takes longer to do most tasks than do experienced employees
   B. One difficult operation takes longer to do than most other operations carried out by the section
   C. A particular employee is very frequently assigned tasks that are not similar and have no relationship to each other
   D. The most highly skilled employee is often assigned the most difficult jobs

   3.____

4. The authority to carry out a job can be delegated to a subordinate, but the supervisor remains responsible for the work of the section as a whole.
   As a supervisor, which of the following rules would be the *BEST* one for you to follow in view of the above statement?

   4.____

A. Avoid assigning important tasks to your subordinates, because you will be blamed if anything goes wrong
B. Be sure each subordinate understands the specific job he has been assigned, and check at intervals to make sure assignments are done properly
C. Assign several people to every important job, so that responsibility will be spread out as much as possible
D. Have an experienced subordinate check all work done by other employees, so that there will be little chance of anything going wrong

5. The human tendency to resist change is often reflected in higher rates of turnover, absenteeism, and errors whenever an important change is made in an organization. Although psychologists do not fully understand the reasons why people resist change, they believe that the resistance stems from a threat to the individual's security, that it is a form of fear of the unknown.
In light of this statement, which one of the following approaches would probably be MOST effective in preparing employees for a change in procedure in their unit?   5._____

A. Avoid letting employees know anything about the change until the last possible moment
B. Sympathize with employees who resent the change and let them know you share their doubts and fears
C. Promise the employees that if the change turns out to be a poor one, you will allow them to suggest a return to the old system
D. Make sure that employees know the reasons for the change and are aware of the benefits that are expected from it

6. Each of the following methods of encouraging employee participation in work planning has been used effectively with different kinds and sizes of employee groups.
Which one of the following methods would be MOST suitable for a group of four technically skilled employees?   6._____

A. Discussions between the supervisor and a representative of the group
B. A suggestion program with semi-annual awards for outstanding suggestions
C. A group discussion summoned whenever a major problem remains unsolved for more than a month
D. Day-to-day exchange of information, opinions and experience

7. Of the following, the MOST important reason why a supervisor is given the authority to tell subordinates what work they should do, how they should do it, and when it should be done is that usually   7._____

A. most people will not work unless there is someone with authority standing over them
B. work is accomplished more effectively if the supervisor plans and coordinates it
C. when division of work is left up to subordinates, there is constant arguing, and very little work is accomplished
D. subordinates are not familiar with the tasks to be performed

8. Fatigue is a factor that affects productivity in all work situations. However, a brief rest period will ordinarily serve to restore a person from fatigue.
According to this statement, which one of the following techniques is most likely to reduce the impact of fatigue on over-all productivity in a unit?   8._____

A. Scheduling several short breaks throughout the day
B. Allowing employees to go home early
C. Extending the lunch period an extra half hour
D. Rotating job assignments every few weeks

9. After giving a new task to an employee, it is a good idea for a supervisor to ask specific questions to make sure that the employee grasps the essentials of the task and sees how it can be carried out. Questions which ask the employee what he thinks or how he feels about an important aspect of the task are particularly effective.
Which one of the following questions is *NOT* the type of question which would be useful in the foregoing situation?

    9.____

A. "Do you feel there will be any trouble meeting the 4:30 deadline?"
B. "How do you feel about the kind of work we do here?"
C. "Do you think that combining those two steps will work all right?"
D. "Can you think of any additional equipment you may need for this process?"

10. Of the following, the *LEAST* important reason for having a *continuous* training program is that

    10.____

A. employees may forget procedures that they have already learned
B. employees may develop short cuts on the job that result in inaccurate work
C. the job continues to change because of new procedures and equipment
D. training is one means of measuring effectiveness and productivity on the job

11. In training a new employee, it is usually advisable to break down the job into meaningful parts and have the new employee master one part before going on to the next.
Of the following, the *BEST* reason for using this technique is to

    11.____

A. let the new employee know the reason for what he is doing and thus encourage him to remain in the unit
B. make the employee aware of the importance of the work and encourage him to work harder
C. show the employee that the work is easy so that he will be encouraged to work faster
D. make it more likely that the employee will experience success and will be encouraged to continue learning the job

12. You may occasionally find a serious error in the work of one of your subordinates.
Of the following, the *BEST* time to discuss such an error with an employee *usually* is

    12.____

A. immediately after the error is found
B. after about two weeks, since you will also be able to point out some good things that the employee has accomplished
C. when you have discovered a pattern of errors on the part of this employee so that he will not be able to dispute your criticism
D. after the error results in a complaint by your own supervisor

13. For very important announcements to the staff, a supervisor should usually use both writ- 13.____
ten and oral communications. For example, when a new procedure is to be introduced,
the supervisor can more easily obtain the group's acceptance by giving his subordinates
a rough draft of the new procedure and calling a meeting of all his subordinates. The
LEAST important benefit of this technique is that it will better enable the supervisor to

    A.   explain why the change is necessary
    B.   make adjustments in the new procedure to meet valid staff objections
    C.   assign someone to carry out the new procedure
    D.   answer questions about the new procedure

14. Assume that, while you are interviewing an individual to obtain information, the individual 14.____
pauses in the middle of an answer.
The *BEST* of the following actions for you to take at that time is to

    A.   correct any inaccuracies in what he has said
    B.   remain silent until he continues
    C.   explain your position on the matter being discussed
    D.   explain that time is short and that he must complete his story quickly

15. When you are interviewing someone to obtain information, the *BEST* of the following rea- 15.____
sons for you to repeat certain of his exact words is to

    A.   assure him that appropriate action will be taken
    B.   encourage him to switch to another topic of discussion
    C.   assure him that you agree with his point of view
    D.   encourage him to elaborate on a point he has made

16. Generally, when writing a letter, the use of precise words and concise sentences is 16.____

    A.   *good,* because less time will be required to write the letter
    B.   *bad,* because it is most likely that the reader will think the letter is unimportant and
       will not respond favorably
    C.   *good,* because it is likely that your desired meaning will be conveyed to the reader
    D.   *bad,* because your letter will be too brief to provide adequate information

17. In which of the following cases would it be *MOST* desirable to have *two* cards for one 17.____
individual in a *single* alphabetic file? The individual has

    A.   a hyphenated surname   B.   two middle names
    C.   a first name with an unusual spelling
    D.   a compound first name

18. Of the following, it is *MOST* appropriate to use a form letter when it is necessary to 18.____
answer many

    A.   requests or inquiries from a single individual
    B.   follow-up letters from individuals requesting additional information
    C.   requests or inquiries about a single subject
    D.   complaints from individuals that they have been unable to obtain various types of
       information

19. Assume that you are asked to make up a budget for your section for the coming year, and you are told that the most important function of the budget is its "control function." Of the following, "control" in this context implies, *most nearly,* that

    A. you will probably be asked to justify expenditures in any category when it looks as though these expenditures are departing greatly from the amount budgeted
    B. your section will probably not be allowed to spend more than the budgeted amount in any given category, although it is always permissible to spend less
    C. your section will be required to spend the exact amount budgeted in every category
    D. the budget will be filed in the Office of the Comptroller so that when the year is over the actual expenditures can be compared with the amounts in the budget

19.____

20. In writing a report, the practice of taking up the *least* important points *first* and the *most* important points *last* is a

    A. *good technique* since the final points made in a report will make the greatest impression on the reader
    B. *good technique* since the material is presented in a more logical manner and will lead directly to the conclusions
    C. *poor technique* since the reader's time is wasted by having to review irrelevant information before finishing the report
    D. *poor technique* since it may cause the reader to lose interest in the report and arrive at incorrect conclusions about the report

20.____

21. Typically, when the technique of "supervision by results" is practiced, higher management sets down, either implicitly or explicitly, certain performance standards or goals that the subordinate is expected to meet. So long as these standards are met, management interferes very little.
The *most likely* result of the use of this technique is that it will

    A. lead to ambiguity in terms of goals
    B. be successful only to the extent that close direct supervision is practiced
    C. make it possible to evaluate both employee and supervisory effectiveness
    D. allow for complete dependence on the subordinate's part

21.____

22. When making written evaluations and reviews of the performance of subordinates, it is *usually ADVISABLE* to

    A. avoid informing the employee of the evaluation if it is critical because it may create hard feelings
    B. avoid informing the employee of the evaluation whether critical or favorable because it is tension-producing
    C. to permit the employee to see the evaluation but not to discuss it with him because the supervisor cannot be certain where the discussion might lead
    D. to discuss the evaluation openly with the employee because it helps the employee understand what is expected of him

22.____

23. There are a number of well-known and respected human relations principles that successful supervisors have been using for years in building good relationships with their employees. Which of the following does *NOT* illustrate such a principle?

23.____

A. Give clear and complete instructions
B. Let each person know how he is getting along
C. Keep an open-door policy
D. Make all relationships personal ones

24. Assume that it is necessary for you to give an unpleasant assignment to one of your sub-ordinates. You expect this employee to raise some objections to this assignment.
The *most appropriate of* the following actions for you to take *FIRST* is to issue the assignment   24.____

    A. *orally,* with the further statement that you will not listen to any complaints
    B. *in writing,* to forestall any complaints by the employee
    C. *orally,* permitting the employee to express his feelings
    D. *in writing,* with a note that any comments should be submitted in writing

25. Suppose you have just announced at a staff meeting with your subordinates that a radical reorganization of work will take place next week. Your subordinates at the meeting appear to be excited, tense, and worried.
Of the following, the *BEST* action for you to take at that time is to   25.____

    A. schedule private conferences with each subordinate to obtain his reaction to the meeting
    B. close the meeting and tell your subordinates to return immediately to their work assignments
    C. give your subordinates some time to ask questions and discuss your announcement
    D. insist that your subordinates do not discuss your announcement among themselves or with other members of the agency

---

KEY (CORRECT ANSWERS)

1. C		11. D	
2. A		12. A	
3. C		13. C	
4. B		14. B	
5. D		15. D	
6. D		16. C	
7. B		17. A	
8. A		18. C	
9. B		19. A	
10. D		20. D	

21. C
22. D
23. D
24. C
25. C

TEST 2

DIRECTIONS: Each question or incomplete statement is followed by several suggested answers or completions. Select the one that *BEST* answer the question or completes the statement. *PRINT THE LETTER OF THE CORRECT ANSWER IN THE SPACE AT THE RIGHT.*

1. Of the following, the *BEST* way for a supervisor to increase employees' interest in their work is to

    A. allow them to make as many decisions as possible
    B. demonstrate to them that he is as technically competent as they
    C. give each employee a difficult assignment
    D. promptly convey to them instructions from higher manage-ment

1.____

2. The *one* of the following which is *LEAST* important in maintaining a high level of productivity on the part of employees is the

    A. provision of optimum physical working conditions for employees
    B. strength of employees' aspirations for promotion
    C. anticipated satisfactions which employees hope to derive from their work
    D. employees' interest in their jobs

2.____

3. Of the following, the *MAJOR* advantage of group problem-solving, as compared to individual problem-solving, is that groups will *more readily*

    A.` abide by their own decisions
    B. agree with agency management
    C. devise new policies and procedures
    D. reach conclusions sooner

3.____

4. The group problem-solving conference is a useful supervisory method for getting people to reach solutions to problems.
Of the following the *reason* that groups usually reach more realistic solutions than do individuals is that

    A. individuals, as a rule, take longer than do groups in reaching decisions and are therefore more likely to make an error
    B. bringing people together to let them confer impresses participants with the seriousness of problems
    C. groups are generally more concerned with the future in evaluating organizational problems
    D. the erroneous opinions of group members tend to be corrected by the other members

4.____

5. A competent supervisor should be able to distinguish between human and technical problems.
Of the following, the *MAJOR* difference between such problems is that serious human problems, in comparison to ordinary technical problems,

    A. are remedied more quickly
    B. involve a lesser need for diagnosis
    C. are more difficult to define
    D. become known through indications which are usually the actual problem

5.____

6. Of the following, the *BEST* justification for a public agency establishing an alcoholism program for its employees is that

    A. alcoholism has traditionally been looked upon with a certain amused tolerance by management and thereby ignored as a serious illness
    B. employees with drinking problems have twice as many on-the-job accidents, especially during the early years of the problem
    C. excessive use of alcohol is associated with personality instability hindering informal social relationships among peers and subordinates
    D. the agency's public reputation will suffer despite an employee's drinking problem being a personal matter of little public concern

6.____

7. Assume you are a manager and you find a group of maintenance employees assigned to your project drinking and playing cards for money in an incinerator room after their regular working hours.
The one of the following actions it would be *BEST* for you to take is to

    A. suspend all employees immediately if there is no question in your mind as to the validity of the charges
    B. review the personnel records of those involved with the supervisor and make a joint decision on which employees should sustain penalties of loss of annual leave or fines
    C. ask the supervisor to interview each violator and submit written reports to you and thereafter consult with the supervisor about disciplinary actions
    D. deduct three days of annual leave from each employee involved if he pleads guilty in lieu of facing more serious charges

7.____

8. Assume that as a manager you must discipline a subordinate, but all of the pertinent facts necessary for a full determination of the appropriate disciplinary action to take are not yet available. However, you fear that a delay in disciplinary action may damage the morale of other employees.
The one of the following which is *MOST* appropriate for you to do in this matter is to

    A. take immediate disciplinary action as if all the pertinent facts were available
    B. wait until all the pertinent facts are available before reaching a decision
    C. inform the subordinate that you know he is guilty, issue a stern warning, and then let him wait for your further act ion
    D. reduce the severity of the discipline appropriate for the violation

8.____

9. There are two standard dismissal procedures utilized by most public agencies. The first is the "open back door" policy, in which the decision of a supervisor in discharging an employee for reasons of inefficiency cannot be cancelled by the central personnel agency. The second is the "closed back door" policy, in which the central personnel agency can order the supervisor to restore the discharged employee to his position.
Of the following, the *major DISADVANTAGE* of the "closed back door" policy as opposed to the "open back door" policy is that central personnel agencies are

    A. likely to approve the dismissal of employees when there is inadequate justification
    B. likely to revoke dismissal actions out of sympathy for employees
    C. less qualified than employing agencies to evaluate the efficiency of employees
    D. easily influenced by political, religious, and racial factors

9.____

10. The one of the following for which a formal grievance-handling system is *LEAST* useful is in   10._____

    A. reducing the frequency of employee complaints
    B. diminishing the likelihood of arbitrary action by supervisors
    C. providing an outlet for employee frustrations
    D. bringing employee problems to the attention of higher management

11. The one of the following managers whose leadership style involves the *GREATEST* delegation of authority to subordinates is the one who presents to subordinates   11._____

    A. his ideas and invites questions
    B. his decision and persuades them to accept it
    C. the problem, gets their suggestions, and makes his decision
    D. a tentative decision which is subject to change

12. Which of the following is *most likely* to cause employee productivity standards to be set too high?   12._____

    A. Standards of productivity are set by first-line supervisors rather than by higher-level managers.
    B. Employees' opinions about productivity standards are sought through written questionnaires.
    C. Initial studies concerning productivity are conducted by staff specialists.
    D. Ideal work conditions assumed in the productivity standards are lacking in actual operations.

13. The one of the following which states the *MAIN* value of an organization chart for a manager is that such charts show the   13._____

    A. lines of formal authority
    B. manner in which duties are performed by each employee
    C. flow of work among employees on the same level
    D. specific responsibilities of each position

14. Which of the following *BEST* names the usual role of a line unit with regard to the organization's programs?   14._____

    A. Seeking publicity   B. Developing
    C. Carrying out   D. Evaluating

15. Critics of promotion *from within* a public agency argue for hiring *from outside* the agency because they believe that promotion from within leads to   15._____

    A. resentment and consequent weakened morale on the part of those not promoted
    B. the perpetuation of outdated practices and policies
    C. a more complex hiring procedure than hiring from outside the agency
    D. problems of objectively appraising someone already in the organization

16. The one of the following management functions which *usually* can be handled *MOST* effectively by a committee is the   16._____

    A. settlement of interdepartmental disputes
    B. planning of routine work schedules
    C. dissemination of information
    D. assignment of personnel

17. Assume that you are serving on a committee which is considering proposals in order to recommend a new maintenance policy. After eliminating a number of proposals by unanimous consent, the committee is deadlocked on three proposals.
The one of the following which is the *BEST* way for the committee to reach agreement on a proposal they could recommend is to

    A. consider and vote on each proposal separately by secret ballot
    B. examine and discuss the three proposals until the proponents of two of them are persuaded they are wrong
    C. reach a synthesis which incorporates the significant features of each proposal
    D. discuss the three proposals until the proponents of each one concede those aspects of the proposals about which there is disagreement

17.____

18. A commonly used training and development method for professional staff is the case method, which utilizes the description of a situation, real or simulated, to provide a common base for analysis, discussion, and problem-solving.
Of the following, the *MOST* appropriate time to use the case method is when professional staff needs

    A. insight into their personality problems
    B. practice in applying management concepts to their own problems
    C. practical experience in the assignment of delegated responsibilities
    D. to know how to function in many different capacities

18.____

19. The incident process is a training and development method in which trainees are given a very brief statement of an event or of a situation presenting a job incident or an employee problem of special significance.
Of the following, it is *MOST* appropriate to use the incident process when

    A. trainees need to learn to review and analyze facts before solving a problem
    B. there are a large number of trainees who require the same information
    C. there are too many trainees to carry on effective discussion
    D. trainees are not aware of the effect of their behavior on others

19.____

20. The one of the following types of information about which a new clerical employee is usually *LEAST* concerned during the orientation process is

    A. his specific job duties
    B. where he will work
    C. his organization's history
    D. who his associates will be

20.____

21. The one of the following which is the *MOST* important limitation on the degree to which work should be broken down into specialized tasks is the point at which

    A. there ceases to be sufficient work of a specialized nature to occupy employees
    B. training costs equal the half-yearly savings derived from further specialization
    C. supervision of employees performing specialized tasks becomes more technical than supervision of general employees
    D. it becomes more difficult to replace the specialist than to replace the generalist who performs a complex set of functions

21.____

22. When a supervisor is asked for his opinion of the suitability for promotion of a subordi-   22.____
nate, the supervisor is actually being asked to predict the subordinate's future behavior in
a new role.
Such a prediction is *most likely* to be accurate if the

    A. higher position is similar to the subordinate's current one
    B. higher position requires intangible personal qualities
    C. new position requires a high intellectual level of performance
    D. supervisor has had little personal association with the subordinate away from the
       job

23. In one form of the non-directive evaluation interview the supervisor communicates his   23.____
evaluation to the employee and then listens to the employee's response without making
further suggestions.
The one of the following which is the *PRINCIPAL* danger of this method of evaluation is
that the employee is most likely to

    A. develop an indifferent attitude towards the supervisor
    B. fail to discover ways of improving his performance
    C. become resistant to change in the organization's structure
    D. place the blame for his shortcomings on his co-workers

24. In establishing rules for his subordinates, a superior should be *PRIMARILY* concerned   24.____
with

    A. creating sufficient flexibility to allow for exceptions
    B. making employees aware of the reasons for the rules and the penalties for infrac-
       tions
    C. establishing the strength of his own position in relation to his subordinates
    D. having his subordinates know that such rules will be imposed in a personal manner

25. The practice of conducting staff training sessions on a periodic basis is *generally* consid-   25.____
ered

    A. *poor;* it takes employees away from their work assignments
    B. *poor;* all staff training should be done on an individual basis
    C. *good;* it permits the regular introduction of new methods and techniques
    D. *good;* it ensures a high employee productivity rate

KEY (CORRECT ANSWERS)

1.	A	11.	C
2.	A	12.	D
3.	A	13.	A
4.	D	14.	C
5.	C	15.	B
6.	B	16.	A
7.	C	17.	C
8.	B	18.	B
9.	C	19.	A
10.	A	20.	C

21.	A
22.	A
23.	B
24.	B
25.	C

EXAMINATION SECTION
TEST 1

DIRECTIONS: Each question or incomplete statement is followed by several suggested answers or completions. Select the one that BEST answers the question or completes the statement. *PRINT THE LETTER OF THE CORRECT ANSWER IN THE SPACE AT THE RIGHT.*

1. Following are three statements concerning on-the-job training:
    I. On-the-job training is rarely used as a method of training employees.
    II. On-the-job training is often carried on with little or no planning.
    III. On-the-job training is often less expensive than other types.
Which of the following BEST classifies the above statements into those that are correct and those that are not?

    A. I is correct, but II and III are not
    B. II is correct, but I and III are not
    C. I and II are correct, but III is not
    D. II and III are correct, but I is not

1.____

2. The one of the following which is NOT a valid principle for a supervisor to keep in mind when talking to a subordinate about his performance is:

    A. People frequently know when they deserve criticism
    B. Supervisors should be prepared to offer suggestions to subordinates about how to improve their work
    C. Good points should be discussed before bad points
    D. Magnifying a subordinate's faults will get him to improve faster

2.____

3. In many organizations information travels quickly through the *grapevine*.
Following are three statements concerning the *grapevine*:
    I. Information a subordinate does not want to tell her supervisor may reach the supervisor through the *grapevine*.
    II. A supervisor can often do her job better by knowing the information that travels through the *grapevine*.
    III. A supervisor can depend on the *grapevine* as a way to get accurate information from the employees on his staff
Which one of the following *correctly* classifies the above statements into those which are generally CORRECT and those which are NOT?

    A. II is correct, but I and III are not
    B. III is correct, but I and II are not
    C. I and II are correct, but III is not
    D. I and III are correct, but II is not

3.____

4. Following are three statements concerning supervision:
    I. A supervisor knows he is doing a good job if his subordinates depend upon him to make every decision.
    II. A supervisor who delegates authority to his subordinates soon finds that his subordinates begin to resent him.
    III. Giving credit for good work is frequently an effective method of getting subordinates to work harder.

4.____

Which one of the following *correctly* classifies the above statements into those that are CORRECT and those that are NOT?

   A. I and II are correct, but III is not
   B. II and III are correct, but I is not
   C. II is correct, but I and III are not
   D. III is correct, but I and II are not

5. Of the following, the LEAST appropriate action for a supervisor to take in preparing a disciplinary case against a subordinate is to   5.___

   A. keep careful records of each incident in which the subordinate has been guilty of misconduct or incompetency, even though immediate disciplinary action may not be necessary
   B. discuss with the employee each incident of misconduct as it occurs so the employee knows where he stands
   C. accept memoranda from any other employees who may have been witnesses to acts of misconduct
   D. keep the subordinate's personnel file confidential so that he is unaware of the evidence being gathered against him

6. Praise by a supervisor can be an important element in motivating subordinates.   6.___
Following are three statements concerning a supervisor's praise of subordinates:
     I. In order to be effective, praise must be lavish and constantly restated.
    II. Praise should be given in a manner which meets the needs of the individual subordinate.
   III. The subordinate whose work is praised should believe that the praise is earned.
Which of the following *correctly* classifies the above statements into those that are CORRECT and those that are NOT?

   A. I is correct, but II and III are not
   B. II and III are correct, but I is not
   C. III is correct, but I and II are not
   D. I and II are correct, but III is not

7. A supervisor feels that he is about to lose his temper while reprimanding a subordinate.   7.___
Of the following, the BEST action for the supervisor to take is to

   A. postpone the reprimand for a short time until his self-control is assured
   B. continue the reprimand because a loss of temper by the supervisor will show the subordinate the seriousness of the error he made
   C. continue the reprimand because failure to do so will show that the supervisor does not have complete self-control
   D. postpone the reprimand until the subordinate is capable of understanding the reason for the supervisor's loss of temper

8. Following are three statements concerning various ways of giving orders to subordinates:

      I.   An implied order or suggestion is usually appropriate for the inexperienced employee.

      II.   A polite request is less likely to upset a sensitive subordinate than a direct order.

      III.   A direct order is usually appropriate in an emergency situation.

Which of the following correctly classifies the above statements into those that are CORRECT and those that are NOT?

    A.   I is correct, but II and III are not
    B.   II and III are correct, but I is not
    C.   III is correct, but I and II are not
    D.   I and II are correct, but III is not

8.____

9. The one of the following which is NOT an acceptable reason for taking disciplinary action against a subordinate guilty of serious violations of the rules is that

    A.   the supervisor can "*let off steam*" against subordinates who break rules frequently
    B.   a subordinate whose work continues to be unsatisfactory may be terminated
    C.   a subordinate may be encouraged to improve his work
    D.   an example is set for other employees

9.____

10. At the first meeting with your staff after appointment as a supervisor, you find considerable indifference and some hostility among the participants.
Of the following, the *most appropriate* way to handle this situation is to

    A.   disregard the attitudes displayed and continue to make your presentation until you have completed it
    B.   discontinue your presentation but continue the meeting and attempt to find out the reasons for their attitudes
    C.   warm up your audience with some good natured statements and anecdotes and then proceed with your presentation
    D.   discontinue the meeting and set up personal interviews with the staff members to try to find out the reason for their attitude

10.____

11. Use a written rather than oral communication to amend any previous written communication.
Of the following, the BEST justification for this statement is that

    A.   oral changes will be considered more impersonal and thus less important
    B.   oral changes will be forgotten or recalled indifferently
    C.   written communications are clearer and shorter
    D.   written communications are better able to convey feeling tone

11.____

12. Assume that a certain supervisor, when writing important communications to his subordinates, often repeats certain points in different words.
This technique is *generally*

    A. *ineffective;* it tends to confuse rather than help
    B. *effective;* it tends to improve understanding by the subordinates
    C. *ineffective;* it unnecessarily increases the length of the communication and may annoy the subordinates
    D. *effective;* repetition is always an advantage in communications

12.____

13. In preparing a letter or a report, a supervisor may wish to persuade the reader of the correctness of some idea or course of action.
The BEST way to accomplish this is for the supervisor to

    A. encourage the reader to make a prompt decision
    B. express each idea in a separate paragraph
    C. present the subject matter of the letter in the first paragraph
    D. state the potential benefits for the reader

13.____

14. Effective communications, a basic necessity for successful supervision is a two-way street. A good supervisor needs to listen to, as well as disseminate, information and he must be able to encourage his subordinates to communicate with him. Which of the following suggestions will contribute LEAST to improving the *listening power* of a supervisor?

    A. Don't assume anything; don't anticipate, and don't let a subordinate think you know what he is going to say
    B. Don't interupt; let him have his full say even if it requires a second session that day to get the full story
    C. React quickly to his statements so that he knows you are interested, even if you must draw some conclusions prematurely
    D. Try to understand the real need for his talking to you even if it is quite different from the subject under discussion

14.____

15. Of the following, the MOST useful approach for the supervisor to take toward the informal employee communications network know as the *grapevine* is to

    A. remain isolated from it, but not take any active steps to eliminate it
    B. listen to it, but not depend on it for accurate information
    C. use it to disseminate confidential information
    D. eliminate it as diplomatically as possible

15.____

16. If a supervisor is asked to estimate the number of employees that he believes he will need in his unit in the coming fiscal year, the supervisor should FIRST attempt to learn the

    A. nature and size of the workload his unit will have during that time
    B. cost of hiring and training new employees
    C. average number of employee absences per year
    D. number of employees needed to indirectly support or assist his unit

16.____

17. An important supervisory responsibility is coordinating the operations of the unit. This   17.____
may include setting work schedules, controlling work quality, establishing interim due
dates, etc. In order to handle this task it has been divided into the following five stages:
    I.   Determine the steps or sequence required for the tasks to be performed.
    II.   Give the orders, either written or oral, to begin work on the Tasks.
    III.   check up by following each task to make sure it is proceeding according to
       plan.
    IV.   Schedule the jobs by setting a time for each task of operation to begin and
       end.
    V.   Control the process by correcting conditions which interfere with the plan.
The MOST logical sequence in which these planning steps should be
performed is

    A. I, II, III, IV, V   B. II, I, V, III, IV
    C. I, IV, II, III, V   D. IV, I, II, III, V

18. Assume that a supervisor calls a meeting with the staff under his supervision in order to   18.____
discuss several proposals. After some discussion, he realizes that he strongly disagrees
with one proposal that four of the staff have rather firmly favored.
At this point, he could BEST handle the situation by saying

    A.   *I have the responsibility for this decision, and I must disagree.*
    B.   *I am just reminding you that I have had a great deal more experience in these
       matters.*
    C.   *You have presented some good points, but perhaps we could look at it another
       way.*
    D.   *The only way that this proposal can be disposed of is to defer it for further discus-
       sion.*

19. As far as the social activities and groups of his subordinates are concerned, a supervisor   19.____
in a large organization can BEST strengthen his tools of leadership by

    A.   emphasizing the organization as a whole and forbidding the formation of groups
    B.   ignoring the groups as much as possible and dealing with each subordinate as an
       individual
    C.   learning about the status structure of employee groups and their values
    D.   avoiding any relationship with groups

20. If a subordinate asks you, his supervisor, for advice in planning his career in the depart-   20.____
ment you *should*

    A.   encourage him to feel that he can easily reach the top of his occupational ladder
    B.   discourage him from setting his hopes too high
    C.   discuss career opportunities realistically with him
    D.   explain that you have no control over his opportunities for advancement

21. A supervisor's evaluation of an employee is usually based upon a combination of objec-   21.____
tive facts and subjective judgments or opinions.
Which of the following aspects of an employee's work or performance is *most likely* to
be subjectively evaluated?

    A. Quantity   B. Accuracy   C. Attitude   D. Attendance

22. Of the following possible characteristics of supervisors, the one *most likely* to lead to failure as a supervisor is

    A. a tendency to seek several opinions before making decisions in complex matters
    B. lack of a strong desire to advance to a top position in management
    C. little formal training in human relations skills
    D. poor relations with subordinates and other supervisory personnel

22.____

23. People who break rules do so for a number of reasons. However, employees will break rules *less* often if

    A. the supervisor uses his own judgment about work methods
    B. the supervisor pretends to act strictly, but isn't really serious about it
    C. they greatly enjoy their work
    D. they have completed many years of service

23.____

24. Assume that an employee under your supervision has become resentful and generally noncooperative after his request for transfer to another office closer to his place of residence was denied. The request was denied primarily because of the importance of his current assignment. The employee has been a valued worker, but you are now worried that his resentful attitude will have a detrimental effect. Of the following, the MOST desirable way for you to handle this situation is to

    A. arrange for the employee's transfer to the office he originally requested
    B. arrange for the employee's transfer to another office, but not the one he originally requested
    C. attempt to re-focus the employee's attention on those aspects of his current assignment which will be most rewarding and satisfying to him
    D. explain to the employee that, while you are sympathetic to his request, department rules will not allow transfers for reasons of personal convenience

24.____

25. Of the following, it would be LEAST advisable for a supervisor to use his administrative authority to affect the behavior and activities of his subordinates when he is trying to

    A. change the way his subordinates perform a particular task
    B. establish a minimum level of conformity to established rules
    C. bring about change in the attitudes of his subordinates
    D. improve the speed with which his subordinates respond to his orders

25.____

26. Assume that a supervisor gives his subordinate instructions which are appropriate and clear. The subordinate thereupon refuses to follow these instructions.
Of the following, it would then be MOST appropriate for the supervisor to

    A. attempt to find out what it is that the employee objects to
    B. take disciplinary action that same day
    C. remind the subordinate about supervisory authority and threaten him with discipline
    D. insist that the subordinate carry out the order immediately

26.____

27. Of the following, the MOST effective way to identify training needs resulting from gradual changes in procedure is to   27.____

    A. monitor on a continuous basis the actual jobs performed and the skills required
    B. periodically send out a written questionnaire asking personnel to identify their needs
    C. conduct interviews at regular intervals with selected employees
    D. consult employees' personnel records

28. Assume that you, as a supervisor, have had a new employee assigned to you. If the duties of his position can be broken into independent parts, which of the following is usually the BEST way to train this new employee?   28.____
Start with

    A. the easiest duties and progressively proceed to the most difficult
    B. something easy; move to something difficult; then back to something easy
    C. something difficult; move to something easy; then to something difficult
    D. the most difficult duties and progressively proceed to the easiest

29. The oldest and most commonly used training technique is on-the-job training. Instruction is given to the worker by his supervisor or by another employee. Such training is essential in most jobs, although it is not always effective when used alone.   29.____
This technique, however, *can* be effectively used alone if

    A. the skills involved can be learned quickly
    B. a large number of people are to be trained at one time
    C. other forms of training have not been previously used with the people involved
    D. the skills to be taught are mental rather than manual

30. It is generally agreed that the learning process is facilitated in proportion to the amount of feedback that the learner is given about his performance.   30.____
Following are three statements concerning the learning process:
    I. The more specific the learner's knowledge of how he performed, the more rapid his improvement and the higher his level of performance.
    II. Giving the learner knowledge of his results does not affect his motivation to learn .
    III. Learners who are not given feedback will set up subjective criteria and evaluate their own performance.
Which of the following choices lists ALL of the above statements that are *generally* correct?

    A. I and II *only*   B. I and III *only*
    C. II and III *only*   D. I, II and III

KEY (CORRECT ANSWERS)

1.	D	11.	B	21.	C
2.	D	12.	B	22.	D
3.	C	13.	D	23.	C
4.	D	14.	C	24.	C
5.	D	15.	B	25.	C
6.	B	16.	A	26.	A
7.	A	17.	C	27.	A
8.	B	18.	C	28.	A
9.	A	19.	C	29.	A
10.	D	20.	C	30.	B

TEST 2

Questions 1–6.

The use of role-playing as a training technique was developed during the past decade by social scientists, particularly psychologists, who have been active in training experiments. Originally, this technique was applied by clinical psychologists who discovered that a patient appears to gain understanding of an emotionally disturbing situation when encouraged to act out roles in that situation. As applied in government and business organizations, the purpose of role-playing is to aid employees to understand certain work problems involving interpersonal relations and to enable observers to evaluate various reactions to them. Thus, for example, on the problem of handling grievances, two individuals from the group might be selected to act out extemporaneously the parts of subordinate and supervisor. When this situation is enacted by various pairs among the class and the techniques and results are discussed, the members of the group are presumed to reach conclusions about the most effective means of handling similar situations. Often the use of role reversal, where participants take parts different from their actual work roles, assists individuals to gain more insight into other people's problems and viewpoints. Although role-playing can be a rewarding training device, the trainer must be aware of his responsibilities. If this technique is to be successful, thorough briefing of both actors and observers as to the situation in question, the participants' roles, and what to look for, is essential.

1. The role-playing technique was FIRST used for the purpose of   1.____

    A. measuring the effectiveness of training programs
    B. training supervisors in business organizations
    C. treating emotionally disturbed patients
    D. handling employee grievances

2. When role-playing is used in private business as a training device, the CHIEF aim is to   2.____

    A. develop better relations between supervisor and subordinate in the handling of grievances
    B. come up with a solution to a specific problem that has arisen
    C. determine the training needs of the group
    D. increase employee understanding of the human relation factors in work situations

3. From the above passage, it is MOST reasonable to conclude that when role-playing is used, it is preferable to have the roles acted out by   3.____

    A. only one set of actors
    B. no more than two sets of actors
    C. several different sets of actors
    D. the trainer or trainers of the group

4. Based on the above passage, a trainer using the technique of role reversal in a problem   4.____
   of first-line supervision should assign a senior employee to play the part of a(n)

   A. new employee   B. senior employee
   C. principal employee   D. angry citizen

5. It can be inferred from the above passage that a limitation of role-play as a training   5.____
   method is that

   A. many work situations do not lend themselves to role-play
   B. employees are not experienced enough as actors to play the roles realistically
   C. only trainers who have psychological training can use it successfully
   D. participants who are observing and not acting do not benefit from it

6. To obtain good results from the use of role-play in training, a trainer should give partici-   6.____
   pants

   A. a minimum of information about the situation so that they can act spontaneously
   B. scripts which illustrate the best method for handling the situation
   C. a complete explanation of the problem and the roles to be acted out
   D. a summary of work problems which involve interpersonal relations

7. Of the following, the MOST important reason for a supervisor to prepare good written   7.____
   reports is that

   A. a supervisor is rated on the quality of his reports
   B. decisions are often made on the basis of the reports
   C. such reports take less time for superiors to review
   D. such reports demonstrate efficiency of department operations

8. Of the following, the BEST test of a good report is whether it   8.____

   A. provides the information needed
   B. shows the good sense of the writer
   C. is prepared according to a proper format
   D. is grammatical and neat

9. When a supervisor writes a report, he can BEST show that he has an understanding of   9.____
   the subject of the report by

   A. including necessary facts and omitting non-essential details
   B. using statistical data
   C. giving his conclusions but not the data on which they are based
   D. using a technical vocabulary

10. Suppose you and another supervisor on the same level are assigned to work together on   10.____
    a report. You disagree strongly with one of the recommendations the other supervisor
    wants to include in the report but you cannot change his views.
    Of the following, it would be BEST that

    A. you refuse to accept responsibility for the report
    B. you ask that someone else be assigned to this project to replace you
    C. each of you state his own ideas about this recommendation in the report
    D. you give in to the other supervisor's opinion for the sake of harmony

11. Standardized forms are often provided for submitting reports.   11.____
Of the following, the MOST important advantage of using standardized forms for
reports is that

    A. they take less time to prepare than individually written reports
    B. necessary information is less likely to be omitted
    C. the responsibility for preparing these reports can be delegated to subordinates
    D. the person making the report can omit information he considers unimportant

12. A report which may BEST be classed as a *periodic* report is one which   12.____

    A. requires the same type of information at regular intervals
    B. contains detailed information which is to be retained in permanent records
    C. is prepared whenever a special situation occurs
    D. lists information in graphic form

13. Which one of the following is NOT an important reason for keeping accurate records in   13.____
an office?

    A. Facts will be on hand when decisions have to be made.
    B. The basis for past actions can be determined.
    C. Information needed by other bureaus can be furnished.
    D. Filing is easier when records are properly made out.

14. Suppose you are preparing to write a report recommending a change in a certain proce-   14.____
dure. You learn that another supervisor made a report a few years ago suggesting a
change in this same procedure, but that no action was taken.
Of the following, it would be MOST desirable for you to

    A. avoid reading the other supervisor's report so that you will write with a more up-to-
date point of view
    B. make no recommendation since management seems to be against any change in
the procedure
    C. read the other report before you write your report to see what bearing it may have
on your recommendations
    D. avoid including in your report any information that can be obtained by referring to
the other report

15. If a report you are preparing to your superior is going to be a very long one, it would be   15.____
DESIRABLE to include a summary of your basic conclusions

    A. at the end of the report
    B. at the beginning of the report
    C. in a separate memorandum
    D. right after you present the supporting data

16. Suppose that some bureau and department policies must be very frequently applied by your subordinates while others rarely come into use.
As a supervising employee, a GOOD technique for you to use in fulfilling your responsibility of seeing to it that policies are adhered to is to

    A. ask the director of the bureau to issue to all employees an explanation in writing of all policies
    B. review with your subordinates every week those policies which have daily application
    C. follow up on and explain at regular intervals the application of those policies which are not used very often by your subordinates
    D. recommend to your superiors that policies rarely used be changed or dropped

16._____

17. The BASIC purpose behind the principle of delegation of authority is to

    A. give the supervisor who is delegating a chance to acquire skills in higher level functions
    B. free the supervisor from routine tasks in order that he may do the important parts of his job
    C. prevent supervisors from overstepping the lines of authority which have been established
    D. place the work delegated in the hands of those employees who can perform it best

17._____

18. A district commander can BEST assist management in long-range planning by

    A. reporting to his superiors any changing conditions in the district
    B. maintaining a neat and efficiently run office
    C. scheduling work so that areas with a high rate of non–compliance get more intensive coverage
    D. properly training new personnel assigned to his district

18._____

19. Suppose that new quarters have been rented for your district office.
Of the following, the LEAST important factor to be considered in planning the layout of the office is the

    A. need for screening confidential activities from unauthorized persons
    B. relative importance of the various types of work
    C. areas of noise concentration
    D. convenience with which communication between sections of the office can be achieved

19._____

20. Of the following, the MOST basic effect of organizing a department so that lines of authority are clearly defined and duties are specifically assigned is to

    A. increase the need for close supervision
    B. decrease the initiative of subordinates
    C. lessen the possibility of duplication of work
    D. increase the responsibilities of supervisory personnel

20._____

21. An accepted management principle is that decisions should be delegated to the lowest point in the organization at which they can be made effectively.
The one of the following which is MOST likely to be a result of the application of this principle is that

    A. no factors will be overlooked in making decisions
    B. prompt action will follow the making of decisions
    C. decisions will be made more rapidly
    D. coordination of decisions that are made will be simplified

21.____

22. Suppose you are a supervisor and need some guidance from a higher authority.
In which one of the following situations would it be PERMISSIBLE for you to bypass the regular upward channels of communication in the chain of command?

    A. In an emergency when your superior is not available
    B. When it is not essential to get a quick reply
    C. When you feel your immediate superior is not understanding of the situation
    D. When you want to obtain information that you think your superior does not have

22.____

23. Of the following, the CHIEF limitation of the organization chart as it is generally used in business and government is that the chart

    A. makes lines of responsibility and authority undesirably definite and formal
    B. is often out of date as soon as it is completed
    C. does not show human factors and informal working relationships
    D. is usually too complicated

23.____

24. The *span of control* for any supervisor is the

    A. number of tasks he is expected to perform himself
    B. amount of office space he and his subordinates occupy
    C. amount of work he is responsible for getting out
    D. number of subordinates he can supervise effectively

24.____

25. Of the following duties performed by a supervising employee, which would be considered a LINE function rather than a staff function?

    A. Evaluation of office personnel
    B. Recommendations for disciplinary action
    C. Initiating budget requests for replacement of equipment
    D. Inspections, at irregular times, of conditions and staff in the field

25.____

KEY (CORRECT ANSWERS)

1.	C	11.	B
2.	D	12.	A
3.	C	13.	D
4.	A	14.	C
5.	A	15.	B
6.	C	16.	C
7.	B	17.	B
8.	A	18.	A
9.	A	19.	B
10.	C	20.	C

21.	B
22.	A
23.	C
24.	D
25.	D

———

PHILOSOPHY, PRINCIPLES, PRACTICES AND TECHNICS
OF
SUPERVISION, ADMINISTRATION, MANAGEMENT AND ORGANIZATION

TABLE OF CONTENTS

TABLE OF CONTENTS (CONTINUED)

PHILOSOPHY, PRINCIPLES, PRACTICES, AND TECHNICS
OF
SUPERVISION, ADMINISTRATION, MANAGEMENT AND ORGANIZATION

I. MEANING OF SUPERVISION

The extension of the democratic philosophy has been accompanied by an extension in the scope of supervision. Modern leaders and supervisors no longer think of supervision in the narrow sense of being confined chiefly to visiting employees, supplying materials, or rating the staff. They regard supervision as being intimately related to all the concerned agencies of society, they speak of the supervisor's function in terms of "growth", rather than the "improvement," of employees.

This modern concept of supervision may be defined as follows:

Supervision is leadership and the development of leadership within groups which are cooperatively engaged in inspection, research, training, guidance and evaluation.

II. THE OLD AND THE NEW SUPERVISION

TRADITIONAL
1. Inspection
2. Focused on the employee
3. Visitation
4. Random and haphazard
5. Imposed and authoritarian
6. One person usually

MODERN
1. Study and analysis
2. Focused on aims, materials, methods, supervisors, employees, environment
3. Demonstrations, intervisitation, workshops, directed reading, bulletins, etc.
4. Definitely organized and planned (scientific)
5. Cooperative and democratic
6. Many persons involved (creative)

III THE EIGHT (8) BASIC PRINCIPLES OF THE NEW SUPERVISION

1. *PRINCIPLE OF RESPONSIBILITY*
   Authority to act and responsibility for acting must be joined.
   a. If you give responsibility, give authority.
   b. Define employee duties clearly.
   c. Protect employees from criticism by others.
   d. Recognize the rights as well as obligations of employees.
   e. Achieve the aims of a democratic society insofar as it is possible within the area of your work.
   f. Establish a situation favorable to training and learning.
   g. Accept ultimate responsibility for everything done in your section, unit, office, division, department.
   h. Good administration and good supervision are inseparable.

2. *PRINCIPLE OF AUTHORITY*
The success of the supervisor is measured by the extent to which the power of authority is not used.

    a. Exercise simplicity and informality in supervision.
    b. Use the simplest machinery of supervision.
    c. If it is good for the organization as a whole, it is probably justified.
    d. Seldom be arbitrary or authoritative.
    e. Do not base your work on the power of position or of personality.
    f. Permit and encourage the free expression of opinions.

3. *PRINCIPLE OF SELF-GROWTH*
The success of the supervisor is measured by the extent to which, and the speed with which, he is no longer needed.

    a. Base criticism on principles, not on specifics.
    b. Point out higher activities to employees.
    c. Train for self-thinking by employees, to meet new situations.
    d. Stimulate initiative, self-reliance and individual responsibility.
    e. Concentrate on stimulating the growth of employees rather than on removing defects.

4. *PRINCIPLE OF INDIVIDUAL WORTH*
Respect for the individual is a paramount consideration in supervision.

    a. Be human and sympathetic in dealing with employees.
    b. Don't nag about things to be done.
    c. Recognize the individual differences among employees and seek opportunities to permit best expression of each personality.

5. *PRINCIPLE OF CREATIVE LEADERSHIP*
The best supervision is that which is not apparent to the employee.

    a. Stimulate, don't drive employees to creative action.
    b. Emphasize doing good things.
    c. Encourage employees to do what they do best.
    d. Do not be too greatly concerned with details of subject or method.
    e. Do not be concerned exclusively with immediate problems and activities.
    f. Reveal higher activities and make them both desired and maximally possible.
    g. Determine procedures in the light of each situation but see that these are derived from a sound basic philosophy.
    h. Aid, inspire and lead so as to liberate the creative spirit latent in all good employees.

6. *PRINCIPLE OF SUCCESS AND FAILURE*
There are no unsuccessful employees, only unsuccessful supervisors who have failed to give proper leadership.

    a. Adapt suggestions to the capacities, attitudes, and prejudices of employees.
    b. Be gradual, be progressive, be persistent.
    c. Help the employee find the general principle; have the employee apply his own problem to the general principle.
    d. Give adequate appreciation for good work and honest effort.
    e. Anticipate employee difficulties and help to prevent them.
    f. Encourage employees to do the desirable things they will do anyway.
    g. Judge your supervision by the results it secures.

7. PRINCIPLE OF SCIENCE

Successful supervision is scientific, objective, and experimental. It is based on facts, not on prejudices.

   a. Be cumulative in results.
   b. Never divorce your suggestions from the goals of training.
   c. Don't be impatient of results.
   d. Keep all matters on a professional, not a personal level.
   e. Do not be concerned exclusively with immediate problems and activities.
   f. Use objective means of determining achicvement and rating where possible.

8. PRINCIPLE OF COOPERATION

Supervision is a cooperative enterprise between supervisor and employee.

   a. Begin with conditions as they are.
   b. Ask opinions of all involved when formulating policies.
   c. Organization is as good as its weakest link.
   d. Let employees help to determine policies and department programs.
   e. Be approachable and accessible - physically and mentally.
   f. Develop pleasant social relationships.

IV. WHAT IS ADMINISTRATION?

Administration is concerned with providing the environment, the material facilities, and the operational procedures that will promote the maximum growth and development of supervisors and employees. (Organization is an aspect, and a concomitant, of administration.)

There is no sharp line of demarcation between supervision and administration; these functions are intimately interrelated and, often, overlapping. They are complementary activities.

1. PRACTICES COMMONLY CLASSED AS "SUPERVISORY"

   a. Conducting employees conferences
   b. Visiting sections, units, offices, divisions, departments
   c. Arranging for demonstrations
   d. Examining plans
   e. Suggesting professional reading
   f. Interpreting bulletins
   g. Recommending in-service training courses
   h. Encouraging experimentation
   i. Appraising employee morale
   j. Providing for intervisitation

2. PRACTICES COMMONLY CLASSIFIED AS "ADMINISTRATIVE"

   a. Management of the office
   b. Arrangement of schedules for extra duties
   c. Assignment of rooms or areas
   d. Distribution of supplies
   e. Keeping records and reports
   f. Care of audio-visual materials
   g. Keeping inventory records
   h. Checking record cards and books
   i. Programming special activities
   j. Checking on the attendance and punctuality of employees

3. *PRACTICES COMMONLY CLASSIFIED AS BOTH "SUPERVISORY" AND "ADMINISTRATIVE"*
   a. Program construction
   b. Testing or evaluating outcomes
   c. Personnel accounting
   d. Ordering instructional materials

V. RESPONSIBILITIES OF THE SUPERVISOR

A person employed in a supervisory capacity must constantly be able to improve his own efficiency and ability. He represents the employer to the employees and only continuous self-examination can make him a capable supervisor.

Leadership and training are the supervisor's responsibility. An efficient working unit is one in which the employees work with the supervisor. It is his job to bring out the best in his employees. He must always be relaxed, courteous and calm in his association with his employees. Their feelings are important, and a harsh attitude does not develop the most efficient employees.

VI. COMPETENCIES OF THE SUPERVISOR

1. Complete knowledge of the duties and responsibilities of his position.
2. To be able to organize a job, plan ahead and carry through.
3. To have self-confidence and initiative.
4. To be able to handle the unexpected situation and make quick decisions.
5. To be able to properly train subordinates in the positions they are best suited for.
6. To be able to keep good human relations among his subordinates.
7. To be able to keep good human relations between his subordinates and himself and to earn their respect and trust.

VII. THE PROFESSIONAL SUPERVISOR-EMPLOYEE RELATIONSHIP

There are two kinds of efficiency: one kind is only apparent and is produced in organizations through the exercise of mere discipline; this is but a simulation of the second, or true, efficiency which springs from spontaneous cooperation. If you are a manager, no matter how great or small your responsibility, it is your job, in the final analysis, to create and develop this involuntary cooperation among the people whom you supervise. For, no matter how powerful a combination of money, machines, and materials a company may have, this is a dead and sterile thing without a team of willing, thinking and articulate people to guide it.

The following 21 points are presented as indicative of the exemplary basic relationship that should exist between supervisor and employee:

1. Each person wants to be liked and respected by his fellow employee and wants to be treated with consideration and respect by his superior.
2. The most competent employee will make an error. However, in a unit where good relations exist between the supervisor and his employees, tenseness and fear do not exist. Thus, errors are not hidden or covered up and the efficiency of a unit is not impaired.
3. Subordinates resent rules, regulations, or orders that are unreasonable or unexplained.
4. Subordinates are quick to resent unfairness, harshness, injustices and favoritism.
5. An employee will accept responsibility if he knows that he will be complimented for a job well done, and not too harshly chastised for failure; that his supervisor will check the cause of the failure, and, if it was the supervisor's fault, he will assume the blame therefore. If it was the employee's fault, his supervisor will explain the correct method or means of handling the responsibility.

6. An employee wants to receive credit for a suggestion he has made, that is used. If a suggestion cannot be used, the employee is entitled to an explanation. The supervisor should not say "no" and close the subject.
7. Fear and worry slow up a worker's ability. Poor working environment can impair his physical and mental health. A good supervisor avoids forceful methods, threats and arguments to get a job done.
8. A forceful supervisor is able to train his employees individually and as a team, and is able to motivate them in the proper channels.
9. A mature supervisor is able to properly evaluate his subordinates and to keep them happy and satisfied.
10. A sensitive supervisor will never patronize his subordinates.
11. A worthy supervisor will respect his employees' confidences.
12. Definite and clear-cut responsibilities should be assigned to each executive.
13. Responsibility should always be coupled with corresponding authority.
14. No change should be made in the scope or responsibilities of a position without a definite understanding to that effect on the part of all persons concerned.
15. No executive or employee, occupying a single position in the organization, should be subject to definite orders from more than one source.
16. Orders should never be given to subordinates over the head of a responsible executive. Rather than do this, the officer in question should be supplanted.
17. Criticisms of subordinates should, whoever possible, be made privately, and in no case should a subordinate be criticized in the presence of executives or employees of equal or lower rank.
18. No dispute or difference between executives or employees as to authority or responsibilities should be considered too trivial for prompt and careful adjudication.
19. Promotions, wage changes, and disciplinary action should always be approved by the executive immediately superior to the one directly responsible.
20. No executive or employee should ever be required, or expected, to be at the same time an assistant to, and critic of, another.
21. Any executive whose work is subject to regular inspection should, whever practicable, be given the assistance and facilities necessary to enable him to maintain an independent check of the quality of his work.

VIII. MINI-TEXT IN SUPERVISION, ADMINISTRATION, MANAGEMENT, AND ORGANIZATION

A. BRIEF HIGHLIGHTS

Listed concisely and sequentially are major headings and important data in the field for quick recall and review.

1. LEVELS OF MANAGEMENT

Any organization of some size has several levels of management. In terms of a ladder the levels are:

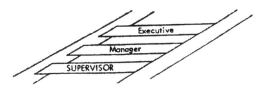

The first level is very important because it is the beginning point of management leadership.

2. WHAT THE SUPERVISOR MUST LEARN

A supervisor must learn to:
 (1) Deal with people and their differences
 (2) Get the job done through people
 (3) Recognize the problems when they exist
 (4) Overcome obstacles to good performance
 (5) Evaluate the performance of people
 (6) Check his own performance in terms of accomplishment

3. A DEFINITION OF SUPERVISOR

The term supervisor means any individual having authority, in the interests of the employer, to hire, transfer, suspend, lay-off, recall, promote, discharge, assign, reward, or discipline other employees or responsibility to direct them, or to adjust their grievances, or effectively to recommend such action, if, in connection with the foregoing, exercise of such authority is not of a merely routine or clerical nature but requires the use of independent judgment.

4. ELEMENTS OF THE TEAM CONCEPT

What is involved in teamwork? The component parts are:
 (1) Members   (3) Goals   (5) Cooperation
 (2) A leader   (4) Plans   (6) Spirit

5. PRINCIPLES OF ORGANIZATION

 (1) A team member must know what his job is.
 (2) Be sure that the nature and scope of a job are understood.
 (3) Authority and responsibility should be carefully spelled out.
 (4) A supervisor should be permitted to make the maximum number of decisions affecting his employees.
 (5) Employees should report to only one supervisor.
 (6) A supervisor should direct only as many employees as he can handle effectively.
 (7) An organization plan should be flexible.
 (8) Inspection and performance of work should be separate.
 (9) Organizational problems should receive immediate attention.
 (10) Assign work in line with ability and experience.

6. THE FOUR IMPORTANT PARTS OF EVERY JOB

 (1) Inherent in every job is the *accountability* for results.
 (2) A second set of factors in every job is *responsibilities*.
 (3) Along with duties and responsibilities one must have the *authority* to act within certain limits without obtaining permission to proceed.
 (4) No job exists in a vacuum. The supervisor is surrounded by key *relationships*.

7. PRINCIPLES OF DELEGATION

Where work is delegated for the first time, the supervisor should think in terms of these questions:
 (1) Who is best qualified to do this?
 (2) Can an employee improve his abilities by doing this?
 (3) How long should an employee spend on this?
 (4) Are there any special problems for which he will need guidance?
 (5) How broad a delegation can I make?

8. PRINCIPLES OF EFFECTIVE COMMUNICATIONS
    (1) Determine the media
    (2) To whom directed?
    (3) Identification and source authority
    (4) Is communication understood?

9. PRINCIPLES OF WORK IMPROVEMENT
    (1) Most people usually do only the work which is assigned to them
    (2) Workers are likely to fit assigned work into the time available to perform it
    (3) A good workload usually stimulates output
    (4) People usually do their best work when they know that results will be reviewed or inspected
    (5) Employees usually feel that someone else is responsible for conditions of work, workplace layout, job methods, type of tools/equipment, and other such factors
    (6) Employees are usually defensive about their job security
    (7) Employees have natural resistance to change
    (8) Employees can support or destroy a supervisor
    (9) A supervisor usually earns the respect of his people through his personal example of diligence and efficiency

10. AREAS OF JOB IMPROVEMENT
The areas of job improvement are quite numerous, but the most common ones which a supervisor can identify and utilize are:

    (1) Departmental layout
    (2) Flow of work
    (3) Workplace layout
    (4) Utilization of manpower
    (5) Work methods
    (6) Materials handling
    (7) Utilization
    (8) Motion economy

11. SEVEN KEY POINTS IN MAKING IMPROVEMENTS
    (1) Select the job to be improved
    (2) Study how it is being done now
    (3) Question the present method
    (4) Determine actions to be taken
    (5) Chart proposed method
    (6) Get approval and apply
    (7) Solicit worker participation

12. CORRECTIVE TECHNIQUES OF JOB IMPROVEMENT

Specific Problems	General Improvement	Corrective Techniques
(1) Size of workload	(1) Departmental layout	(1) Study with scale model
(2) Inability to meet schedules	(2) Flow of work	(2) Flow chart study
(3) Strain and fatigue	(3) Work plan layout	(3) Motion analysis
(4) Improper use of men and skills	(4) Utilization of manpower	(4) Comparison of units produced to standard allowance
(5) Waste, poor quality, unsafe conditions	(5) Work methods	(5) Methods analysis
(6) Bottleneck conditions that hinder output	(6) Materials handling	(6) Flow chart & equipment study
(7) Poor utilization of equipment and machine	(7) Utilization of equipment	(7) Down time vs. running time
(8) Efficiency and productivity of labor	(8) Motion economy	(8) Motion analysis

13. A *PLANNING CHECKLIST*

(1) Objectives	(6) Resources	(11) Safety
(2) Controls	(7) Manpower	(12) Money
(3) Delegations	(8) Equipment	(13) Work
(4) Communications	(9) Supplies and materials	(14) Timing of improvements
(5) Resources	(10) Utilization of time	

14. *FIVE CHARACTERISTICS OF GOOD DIRECTIONS*

In order to get results, directions must be:

(1) Possible of accomplishment	(3) Related to mission	(5) Unmistakably clear
(2) Agreeable with worker interests	(4) Planned and complete	

15. *TYPES OF DIRECTIONS*

(1) Demands or direct orders	(3) Suggestion or implication
(2) Requests	(4) Volunteering

16. *CONTROLS*

A typical listing of the overall areas in which the supervisor should establish controls might be:

(1) Manpower	(3) Quality of work	(5) Time	(7) Money
(2) Materials	(4) Quantity of work	(6) Space	(8) Methods

17. *ORIENTING THE NEW EMPLOYEE*

(1) Prepare for him	(3) Orientation for the job
(2) Welcome the new employee	(4) Follow-up

18. *CHECKLIST FOR ORIENTING NEW EMPLOYEES*   Yes   No

(1) Do your appreciate the feelings of new employees when they first report for work?   ____ ____

(2) Are you aware of the fact that the new employee must make a big adjustment to his job?   ____ ____

(3) Have you given him good reasons for liking the job and the organization?   ____ ____

(4) Have you prepared for his first day on the job?

(5) Did you welcome him cordially and make him feel needed?

(6) Did you establish rapport with him so that he feels free to talk and discuss matters with you?

(7) Did you explain his job to him and his relationship to you?   ____ ____

(8) Does he know that his work will be evaluated periodically on a basis that is fair and objective?   ____ ____

(9) Did you introduce him to his fellow workers in such a way that they are likely to accept him?   ____ ____

(10) Does he know what employee benefits he will receive?

(11) Does he understand the importance of being on the job and what to do if he must leave his duty station?   ____ ____

(12) Has he been impressed with the importance of accident prevention and safe practice?   ____ ____

(13) Does he generally know his way around the department?   ____ ____

(14) Is he under the guidance of a sponsor who will teach the right ways of doing things?   ____ ____

(15) Do you plan to follow-up so that he will continue to adjust successfully to his job?   ____ ____

19. *PRINCIPLES OF LEARNING*
      (1) Motivation   (2) Demonstration or explanation   (3) Practice

20. *CAUSES OF POOR PERFORMANCE*
      (1) Improper training for job
      (2) Wrong tools
      (3) Inadequate directions
      (4) Lack of supervisory follow-up
      (5) Poor communications
      (6) Lack of standards of performance
      (7) Wrong work habits
      (8) Low morale
      (9) Other

21. *FOUR MAJOR STEPS IN ON-THE-JOB INSTRUCTION*
      (1) Prepare the worker
      (2) Present the operation
      (3) Tryout performance
      (4) Follow-up

22. *EMPLOYEES WANT FIVE THINGS*
      (1) Security (2) Opportunity (3) Recognition (4) Inclusion (5) Expression

23. *SOME DON'TS IN REGARD TO PRAISE*
      (1) Don't praise a person for something he hasn't done
      (2) Don't praise a person unless you can be sincere
      (3) Don't be sparing in praise just because your superior withholds it from you
      (4) Don't let too much time elapse between good performance and recognition of it

24. *HOW TO GAIN YOUR WORKERS' CONFIDENCE*
    Methods of developing confidence include such things as:
      (1) Knowing the interests, habits, hobbies of employees
      (2) Admitting your own inadequacies
      (3) Sharing and telling of confidence in others
      (4) Supporting people when they are in trouble
      (5) Delegating matters that can be well handled
      (6) Being frank and straightforward about problems and working conditions
      (7) Encouraging others to bring their problems to you
      (8) Taking action on problems which impede worker progress

25. *SOURCES OF EMPLOYEE PROBLEMS*
    On-the-job causes might be such things as:
      (1) A feeling that favoritism is exercised in assignments
      (2) Assignment of overtime
      (3) An undue amount of supervision
      (4) Changing methods or systems
      (5) Stealing of ideas or trade secrets
      (6) Lack of interest in job
      (7) Threat of reduction in force
      (8) Ignorance or lack of communications
      (9) Poor equipment
      (10) Lack of knowing how supervisor feels toward employee
      (11) Shift assignments

    Off-the-job problems might have to do with:
      (1) Health   (2) Finances   (3) Housing   (4) Family

26. *THE SUPERVISOR'S KEY TO DISCIPLINE*

There are several key points about discipline which the supervisor should keep in mind:

(1) Job discipline is one of the disciplines of life and is directed by the supervisor.

(2) It is more important to correct an employee fault than to fix blame for it.

(3) Employee performance is affected by problems both on the job and off.

(4) Sudden or abrupt changes in behavior can be indications of important employee problems.

(5) Problems should be dealt with as soon as possible after they are identified.

(6) The attitude of the supervisor may have more to do with solving problems than the techniques of problem solving.

(7) Correction of employee behavior should be resorted to only after the supervisor is sure that training or counseling will not be helpful.

(8) Be sure to document your disciplinary actions.

(9) Make sure that you are disciplining on the basis of facts rather than personal feelings.

(10) Take each disciplinary step in order, being careful not to make snap judgments, or decisions based on impatience.

27. *FIVE IMPORTANT PROCESSES OF MANAGEMENT*

(1) Planning   (2) Organizing   (3) Scheduling

(4) Controlling   (5) Motivating

28. *WHEN THE SUPERVISOR FAILS TO PLAN*

(1) Supervisor creates impression of not knowing his job

(2) May lead to excessive overtime

(3) Job runs itself -- supervisor lacks control

(4) Deadlines and appointments missed

(5) Parts of the work go undone

(6) Work interrupted by emergencies

(7) Sets a bad example

(8) Uneven workload creates peaks and valleys

(9) Too much time on minor details at expense of more important tasks

29. *FOURTEEN GENERAL PRINCIPLES OF MANAGEMENT*

(1) Division of work

(2) Authority and responsibility

(3) Discipline

(4) Unity of command

(5) Unity of direction

(6) Subordination of individual interest to general interest

(7) Remuneration of personnel

(8) Centralization

(9) Scalar chain

(10) Order

(11) Equity

(12) Stability of tenure of personnel

(13) Initiative

(14) Esprit de corps

30. *CHANGE*

Bringing about change is perhaps attempted more often, and yet less well understood, than anything else the supervisor does. How do people generally react to change? (People tend to resist change that is imposed upon them by other individuals or circumstances.

Change is characteristic of every situation. It is a part of every real endeavor where the efforts of people are concerned.

A. Why do people resist change?

    People may resist change because of:

        (1) Fear of the unknown

        (2) Implied criticism

        (3) Unpleasant experiences in the past

        (4) Fear of loss of status

        (5) Threat to the ego

        (6) Fear of loss of economic stability

B. How can we best overcome the resistance to change?

    In initiating change, take these steps:

        (1) Get ready to sell

        (2) Identify sources of help

        (3) Anticipate objections

        (4) Sell benefits

        (5) Listen in depth

        (6) Follow up

B. BRIEF TOPICAL SUMMARIES

I. WHO/WHAT IS THE SUPERVISOR?

1. The supervisor is often called the "highest level employee and the lowest level manager."
2. A supervisor is a member of both management and the work group. He acts as a bridge between the two.
3. Most problems in supervision are in the area of human relations, or people problems.
4. Employees expect: Respect, opportunity to learn and to advance, and a sense of belonging, and so forth.
5. Supervisors are responsible for directing people and organizing work. Planning is of paramount importance.
6. A position description is a set of duties and responsibilities inherent to a given position.
7. It is important to keep the position description up-to-date and to provide each employee with his own copy.

II. THE SOCIOLOGY OF WORK

1. People are alike in many ways; however, each individual is unique.
2. The supervisor is challenged in getting to know employee differences. Acquiring skills in evaluating individuals is an asset.
3. Maintaining meaningful working relationships in the organization is of great importance.
4. The supervisor has an obligation to help individuals to develop to their fullest potential.
5. Job rotation on a planned basis helps to build versatility and to maintain interest and enthusiasm in work groups.
6. Cross training (job rotation) provides backup skills.
7. The supervisor can help reduce tension by maintaining a sense of humor, providing guidance to employees, and by making reasonable and timely decisions. Employees respond favorably to working under reasonably predictable circumstances.
8. Change is characteristic of all managerial behavior. The supervisor must adjust to changes in procedures, new methods, technological changes, and to a number of new and sometimes challenging situations.
9. To overcome the natural tendency for people to resist change, the supervisor should become more skillful in initiating change.

III. PRINCIPLES AND PRACTICES OF SUPERVISION

1. Employees should be required to answer to only one superior.
2. A supervisor can effectively direct only a limited number of employees, depending upon the complexity, variety, and proximity of the jobs involved.
3. The organizational chart presents the organization in graphic form. It reflects lines of authority and responsibility as well as interrelationships of units within the organization.
4. Distribution of work can be improved through an analysis using the "Work Distribution Chart."
5. The "Work Distribution Chart" reflects the division of work within a unit in understandable form.
6. When related tasks are given to an employee, he has a better chance of increasing his skills through training.
7. The individual who is given the responsibility for tasks must also be given the appropriate authority to insure adequate results.
8. The supervisor should delegate repetitive, routine work. Preparation of recurring reports, maintaining leave and attendance records are some examples.
9. Good discipline is essential to good task performance. Discipline is reflected in the actions of employees on the job in the absence of supervision.
10. Disciplinary action may have to be taken when the positive aspects of discipline have failed. Reprimand, warning, and suspension are examples of disciplinary action.
11. If a situation calls for a reprimand, be sure it is deserved and remember it is to be done in private.

IV. DYNAMIC LEADERSHIP

1. A style is a personal method or manner of exerting influence.
2. Authoritarian leaders often see themselves as the source of power and authority.
3. The democratic leader often perceives the group as the source of authority and power.
4. Supervisors tend to do better when using the pattern of leadership that is most natural for them.
5. Social scientists suggest that the effective supervisor use the leadership style that best fits the problem or circumstances involved.
6. All four styles -- telling, selling, consulting, joining -- have their place. Using one does not preclude using the other at another time.
7. The theory X point of view assumes that the average person dislikes work, will avoid it whenever possible, and must be coerced to achieve organizational objectives.
8. The theory Y point of view assumes that the average person considers work to be as natural as play, and, when the individual is committed, he requires little supervision or direction to accomplish desired objectives.
9. The leader's basic assumptions concerning human behavior and human nature affect his actions, decisions, and other managerial practices.
10. Dissatisfaction among employees is often present, but difficult to isolate. The supervisor should seek to weaken dissatisfaction by keeping promises, being sincere and considerate, keeping employees informed, and so forth.
11. Constructive suggestions should be encouraged during the natural progress of the work.

V. PROCESSES FOR SOLVING PROBLEMS

1. People find their daily tasks more meaningful and satisfying when they can improve them.
2. The causes of problems, or the key factors, are often hidden in the background. Ability to solve problems often involves the ability to isolate them from their backgrounds. There is some substance to the cliché that some persons "can't see the forest for the trees."
3. New procedures are often developed from old ones. Problems should be broken down into manageable parts. New ideas can be adapted from old ones.

4. People think differently in problem-solving situations. Using a logical, patterned approach is often useful. One approach found to be useful includes these steps:

    (a) Define the problem   (d) Weigh and decide

    (b) Establish objectives   (e) Take action

    (c) Get the facts   (f) Evaluate action

VI. TRAINING FOR RESULTS

1. Participants respond best when they feel training is important to them.
2. The supervisor has responsibility for the training and development of those who report to him.
3. When training is delegated to others, great care must be exercised to insure the trainer has knowledge, aptitude, and interest for his work as a trainer.
4. Training (learning) of some type goes on continually. The most successful supervisor makes certain the learning contributes in a productive manner to operational goals.
5. New employees are particularly susceptible to training. Older employees facing new job situations require specific training, as well as having need for development and growth opportunities.
6. Training needs require continuous monitoring.
7. The training officer of an agency is a professional with a responsibility to assist supervisors in solving training problems.
8. Many of the self-development steps important to the supervisor's own growth are equally important to the development of peers and subordinates. Knowledge of these is important when the supervisor consults with others on development and growth opportunities.

VII. HEALTH, SAFETY, AND ACCIDENT PREVENTION

1. Management-minded supervisors take appropriate measures to assist employees in maintaining health and in assuring safe practices in the work environment.
2. Effective safety training and practices help to avoid injury and accidents.
3. Safety should be a management goal. All infractions of safety which are observed should be corrected without exception.
4. Employees' safety attitude, training and instruction, provision of safe tools and equipment, supervision, and leadership are considered highly important factors which contribute to safety and which can be influenced directly by supervisors.
5. When accidents do occur they should be investigated promptly for very important reasons, including the fact that information which is gained can be used to prevent accidents in the future.

VIII. EQUAL EMPLOYMENT OPPORTUNITY

1. The supervisor should endeavor to treat all employees fairly, without regard to religion, race, sex, or national origin.
2. Groups tend to reflect the attitude of the leader. Prejudice can be detected even in very subtle form. Supervisors must strive to create a feeling of mutual respect and confidence in every employee.
3. Complete utilization of all human resources is a national goal. Equitable consideration should be accorded women in the work force, minority-group members, the physically and mentally handicapped, and the older employee. The important question is: "Who can do the job?"
4. Training opportunities, recognition for performance, overtime assignments, promotional opportunities, and all other personnel actions are to be handled on an equitable basis.

IX. IMPROVING COMMUNICATIONS

1. Communications is achieving understanding between the sender and the receiver of a message. It also means sharing information -- the creation of understanding.
2. Communication is basic to all human activity. Words are means of conveying meanings; however, real meanings are in people.
3. There are very practical differences in the effectiveness of one-way, impersonal, and two-way communications. Words spoken face-to-face are better understood. Telephone conversations are effective, but lack the rapport of person-to-person exchanges. The whole person communicates.
4. Cooperation and communication in an organization go hand in hand. When there is a mutual respect between people, spelling out rules and procedures for communicating is unnecessary.
5. There are several barriers to effective communications. These include failure to listen with respect and understanding, lack of skill in feedback, and misinterpreting the meanings of words used by the speaker. It is also common practice to listen to what we want to hear, and tune out things we do not want to hear.
6. Communication is management's chief problem. The supervisor should accept the challenge to communicate more effectively and to improve interagency and intra-agency communications.
7. The supervisor may often plan for and conduct meetings. The planning phase is critical and may determine the success or the failure of a meeting.
8. Speaking before groups usually requires extra effort. Stage fright may never disappear completely, but it can be controlled.

X. SELF-DEVELOPMENT

1. Every employee is responsible for his own self-development.
2. Toastmaster and toastmistress clubs offer opportunities to improve skills in oral communications.
3. Planning for one's own self-development is of vital importance. Supervisors know their own strengths and limitations better than anyone else.
4. Many opportunities are open to aid the supervisor in his developmental efforts, including job assignments; training opportunities, both governmental and non-governmental -- to include universities and professional conferences and seminars.
5. Programmed instruction offers a means of studying at one's own rate.
6. Where difficulties may arise from a supervisor's being away from his work for training, he may participate in televised home study or correspondence courses to meet his self-develop- ment needs.

XI. TEACHING AND TRAINING

A. The Teaching Process

Teaching is encouraging and guiding the learning activities of students toward established goals. In most cases this process consists in five steps: preparation, presentation, summarization, evaluation, and application.

1. Preparation

Preparation is twofold in nature; that of the supervisor and the employee.

Preparation by the supervisor is absolutely essential to success. He must know what, when, where, how, and whom he will teach. Some of the factors that should be considered are:

(1) The objectives	(5) Employee interest
(2) The materials needed	(6) Training aids
(3) The methods to be used	(7) Evaluation
(4) Employee participation	(8) Summarization

Employee preparation consists in preparing the employee to receive the material. Probably the most important single factor in the preparation of the employee is arousing and maintaining his interest. He must know the objectives of the training, why he is there, how the material can be used, and its importance to him.

2. Presentation

In presentation, have a carefully designed plan and follow it.
The plan should be accurate and complete, yet flexible enough to meet situations as they arise. The method of presentation will be determined by the particular situation and objectives.

3. Summary

A summary should be made at the end of every training unit and program. In addition, there may be internal summaries depending on the nature of the material being taught. The important thing is that the trainee must always be able to understand how each part of the new material relates to the whole.

4. Application

The supervisor must arrange work so the employee will be given a chance to apply new knowledge or skills while the material is still clear in his mind and interest is high. The trainee does not really know whether he has learned the material until he has been given a chance to apply it. If the material is not applied, it loses most of its value.

5. Evaluation

The purpose of all training is to promote learning. To determine whether the training has been a success or failure, the supervisor must evaluate this learning.

In the broadest sense evaluation includes all the devices, methods, skills, and techniques used by the supervisor to keep him self and the employees informed as to their progress toward the objectives they are pursuing. The extent to which the employee has mastered the knowledge, skills, and abilities, or changed his attitudes, as determined by the program objectives, is the extent to which instruction has succeeded or failed.

Evaluation should not be confined to the end of the lesson, day, or program but should be used continuously. We shall note later the way this relates to the rest of the teaching process.

B. Teaching Methods

A teaching method is a pattern of identifiable student and instructor activity used in presenting training material.

All supervisors are faced with the problem of deciding which method should be used at a given time.

As with all methods, there are certain advantages and disadvantages to each method.

1. Lecture

The lecture is direct oral presentation of material by the supervisor. The present trend is to place less emphasis on the trainer's activity and more on that of the trainee.

2. Discussion

Teaching by discussion or conference involves using questions and other techniques to arouse interest and focus attention upon certain areas, and by doing so creating a learning situation. This can be one of the most valuable methods because it gives the employees 'an opportunity to express their ideas and pool their knowledge.

3. Demonstration

    The demonstration is used to teach how something works or how to do something. It can be used to show a principle or what the results of a series of actions will be. A well-staged demonstration is particularly effective because it shows proper methods of performance in a realistic manner.

4. Performance

    Performance is one of the most fundamental of all learning techniques or teaching methods. The trainee may be able to tell how a specific operation should be performed but he cannot be sure he knows how to perform the operation until he has done so.

5. Which Method to Use

    Moreover, there are other methods and techniques of teaching. It is difficult to use any method without other methods entering into it. In any learning situation a combination of methods is usually more effective than anyone method alone.

Finally, evaluation must be integrated into the other aspects of the teaching-learning process.

It must be used in the motivation of the trainees; it must be used to assist in developing understanding during the training; and it must be related to employee application of the results of training.

This is distinctly the role of the supervisor.

Made in the USA
Middletown, DE
28 September 2021